FROM ROOKIE TO RAINMAKER

The Ultimate Sales Playbook Rooted in Ancient Wisdom

Ashutosh Pathak

BlueRose ONE.com
Stories Matter
NewDelhi • London

BLUEROSE PUBLISHERS
India | U.K.

BlueRose ONE
Stories Matter
NewDelhi • London

For permissions requests or inquiries regarding this publication, please contact:

BLUEROSE PUBLISHERS
www.BlueRoseONE.com
info@bluerosepublishers.com
+91 8882 898 898
+4407342408967

ISBN: 978-93-7018-382-7

Cover design: Shubham Verma
Typesetting: Sagar

First Edition: April 2025

About the Author

Ashutosh Pathak is a dynamic **Corporate Trainer, Senior Trainer,** and **transformation coach** with over 12 years of distinguished experience in the Corporate Training, insurance and financial services industry. Known for his remarkable ability to energize, uplift, and empower professionals, he has trained and mentored thousands of advisors, frontline sales professionals, sales leaders, and training managers across India in the domains of **sales excellence, leadership development, and behavioral transformation**.

He brings a rare blend of **spiritual wisdom and modern sales science** to his training approach. A strong believer in the power of ancient Indian texts like the Bhagavad Gita and Ramayana, Ashutosh weaves timeless principles into practical tools for today's sales world. His sessions are deeply immersive, transformational, and purpose-driven—designed not just to boost performance, but to create mindful, ethical, and inspired professionals.

He is also a **MORD-certified trainer**, recognized for his credible contribution to capacity building and developmental learning initiatives.

Ashutosh has been honored with several prestigious accolades:

- **Extra Mile Champion** – Beyond the Call of Duty
- **Best Trainer Award** – For outstanding facilitation and impact
- **Commitment Value Champion** – For embodying excellence and perseverance
- **I M ABC – Be Collaborative Award** – For fostering a culture of growth and synergy

This book is a reflection of his mission: to transform ordinary salespeople into extraordinary Rainmakers who lead with authenticity, live with purpose, and sell with soul

About the Book

Success is a game of influence, persuasion, and resilience—whether you're closing a deal, leading a team, or simply navigating life's challenges. From Rookie to Rainmaker: The Ultimate Sales Playbook Rooted in Ancient Wisdom is more than just a sales book; it's a transformational guide that blends time-tested principles from the Bhagavad Gita, Ramayana, and other ancient texts with modern sales strategies.

Whether you're a seasoned salesperson, an entrepreneur, or someone looking to master the art of communication and decision-making, this book equips you with powerful lessons on mindset, persuasion, negotiation, and storytelling. Packed with actionable techniques, real-world case studies, and profound insights, it will help you unlock your full potential—both professionally and personally.

Master the timeless principles of success and become a Rainmaker in every aspect of life!

Foreword -

Mr Ayan Chatterjee - Head Sales Training (Aditya Birla Capital- ABSLI)

What is sales? Is it an Art or a science? This debate will never stop. However, people like us, who are sales professionals by heart, always feel that there is a sales man in each one of us.

Rookie to Rainmaker is a beautiful effort to answer your questions about how to be a successful sales professional.

But there are a lot of books around the same. How is this book different?

This book tried to answer your questions, not only with theories but it also tried to bring in age old wisdom from ancient literature to validate these points.

The book is divided into 20 chapters and each chapter will talk about concepts, examples, references from ancient literature and will help you plan execution action items.

Ashutosh is an exemplary sales trainer and who can train you better on Sales concepts than a master Sales trainer.

Read, deep dive, reflect and enjoy your reading. While you get soaked in learning, here is wishing **Ashutosh** all the best in his literary endeavour.

Who this book is for

This book is for:

✔ Aspiring sales professionals who want to master the art of selling from day one.

✔ Experienced salespeople looking to sharpen their skills and elevate their performance.

✔ Entrepreneurs and business owners who need to sell their products and ideas with confidence.

✔ Sales leaders and managers who want to build high-performing teams and create a culture of sales excellence.

✔ Anyone looking for a blend of modern sales techniques and timeless wisdom to achieve peak success in their career.

If you've ever felt stuck in sales, struggled with objections, or wanted a clear, actionable roadmap to sales mastery—this book is for you.

- **How to use this book**

This book is structured as a step-by-step guide to help you go from a rookie to a rainmaker. Each chapter is packed with:

- ❖ Powerful sales strategies that you can apply immediately.
- ❖ Real-life case studies to help you understand the concepts in action.
- ❖ Timeless lessons from ancient scriptures that provide deep insights into human psychology and influence.
- ❖ Actionable exercises and assignments to ensure that you don't just read—but implement.

The best way to use this book? Read, reflect, and take action. Apply the learnings, practice consistently, and watch your sales results transform.

- **What makes this book different**

Unlike traditional sales books that focus solely on techniques, this book:

✅ Combines modern sales strategies with ancient wisdom from the Bhagavad Gita, Ramayana, Vedas, and Puranas.

✅ Focuses on mindset, psychology, and influence—not just scripts and pitches.

✅ Provides practical, battle-tested strategies that work in the real world.

✅ Helps you become not just a successful salesperson but a sales leader.

✅ Offers exercises, assignments, and real-world applications for long-term mastery.

This is not just a book—it's a blueprint to becoming a top-performing sales professional.

- **Structure and approach**

This book is structured to provide both strategic insights and actionable steps to help you become a Rainmaker—a top-performing salesperson who consistently delivers results.

Each chapter follows a practical, easy-to-apply format:

✔ Key Concept: Introduction to a crucial sales principle.

✔ Ancient Wisdom: Lessons from the Bhagavad Gita, Ramayana, Vedas, and Puranas on sales, persuasion, and leadership.

✔ Real-World Applications: Case studies and practical

examples.

✔ Proven Strategies: Step-by-step techniques you can apply immediately.

✔ Exercises & Key Takeaways: Actionable insights to reinforce learning.

This book blends timeless wisdom with modern sales science, giving you a unique edge in today's competitive world. Whether you're a beginner or a seasoned professional, you can read it sequentially or jump to specific chapters based on your needs.

Now, let's begin your transformation into a Rainmaker

Introduction: The Path to Becoming a Rainmaker

- **What is a Rainmaker?**

In the world of sales, a rainmaker is someone who consistently brings in high-value deals, commands respect, and possesses an almost mystical ability to turn prospects into loyal customers. They are not just skilled salespeople; they are influencers, problem-solvers, and masters of persuasion.

A rainmaker doesn't rely on luck. They operate with clarity, strategy, and unshakable confidence—qualities that are cultivated through knowledge, discipline, and experience.

But what truly sets them apart?

1. They understand human psychology and the deeper motivations behind a purchase.

2. They build relationships that last—turning customers into lifelong clients.

3. They operate with a warrior's mindset—focused, determined, and adaptable.

4. They follow a structured sales process but add their own unique style to stand out.

A rainmaker is not just someone who sells. They inspire trust, deliver value, and create an impact.

- **Why sales is an art and a science**

Sales is often misunderstood as a game of manipulation or persuasion. In reality, it is a perfect blend of art and science.

- The art of sales lies in building rapport, telling compelling stories, and adapting to different personalities.
- The science of sales is in understanding buying psychology, following a structured process, and using data to make better decisions.

A successful salesperson knows when to analyze the numbers and when to trust their instincts. They learn from their failures, refine their approach, and consistently push themselves to improve.

- **How ancient wisdom can shape modern sales success**

Ancient Wisdom: The Missing Link in Modern Sales

What if the secrets to becoming an unstoppable salesperson were already written thousands of years ago?

Sales is, at its core, about influence, trust, and human connection—principles deeply embedded in ancient Indian scriptures. The Bhagavad Gita, Ramayana, Vedas, and Puranas provide timeless lessons on leadership, decision-making, communication, and persuasion, all of which are critical for mastering sales.

For example, in the Bhagavad Gita (2.47),

Lord Krishna teaches:

कर्मण्येवाधिकारस्ते मा फलेषु कदाचन।
मा कर्मफलहेतुर्भूर्मा ते सङ्गोऽस्त्वकर्मणि॥

"Your right is to perform your duty only, but never to its fruits. Do not be driven by the results, nor be attached to inaction."

This shloka is a powerful principle for sales professionals. It teaches us that our job is to give our best effort, stay consistent, and focus on the process—without being overly attached to immediate results. The best salespeople don't chase outcomes; they master the process, and the results follow naturally.

Similarly, in the Ramayana, Lord Hanuman is a perfect example of confidence, communication, and unwavering commitment—qualities that every sales professional should embody. When he meets Sita in Lanka, he wins her trust through his sincerity, knowledge, and clarity of speech—a lesson in effective communication for all salespeople.

By integrating these timeless teachings with modern sales strategies, this book offers a unique, powerful, and transformative approach to mastering sales.

Table of Contents

Chapter 1: The Mindset of a Rainmaker

- Cultivate a winning mindset rooted in inner strength.
- Overcome self-doubt using timeless teachings from the Bhagavad Gita.
- Learn habits that define top sales performers.

Chapter 2: Lakshya – The Art of Goal Setting, the Warrior Way

- Set powerful, crystal-clear goals with laser-sharp focus.
- Channel the discipline of Arjuna and ancient warriors.
- Blend intention, purpose, and action for success.

Chapter 3: The Art and Science of Sales – Balancing Emotion and Strategy for Maximum Success

- Discover how successful selling balances heart and logic.
- Learn when to lead with emotion vs. strategy.
- Apply Vedic wisdom to structure a powerful sales approach.

Chapter 4: Mastering the Sales Process—From First Contact to Closing the Deal

- Understand each stage of the sales journey.
- Navigate prospecting, pitching, follow-ups, and closing with precision.
- Avoid common pitfalls with step-by-step guidance.

Chapter 5: The Art of Prospecting – How to Find and Attract High-Quality Leads

- Use proven prospecting strategies that generate results.
- Learn the spiritual laws of attraction and alignment.
- Build a consistent, high-converting sales pipeline.

Chapter 6: The Psychology of Selling – How to Influence and Persuade Anyone

- Understand what drives customer decisions.
- Use subtle psychological triggers and ethical influence.
- Blend neuroscience and ancient insights for maximum impact.

Chapter 7: The Power of Storytelling in Sales – How to Win Hearts and Close Deals

- Craft compelling sales narratives that connect emotionally.
- Use storytelling techniques inspired by epics like the Ramayana.
- Position yourself and your product as the hero's guide.

Chapter 8: Sealing the Deal – A Step-by-Step Guide to Winning Sales Like a Warrior

- Recognize buying signals and perfect your timing.
- Learn proven closing techniques.
- Overcome last-minute objections with calm confidence.

Chapter 9: Mastering Objection Handling – Turning 'No' into 'Yes'

- Decode the real meaning behind client objections.
- Learn practical, powerful objection-handling frameworks.
- Use the Mahabharata's lessons to turn resistance into results.

Chapter 10: Building Long-Term Client Relationships for Repeat Sales and Referrals

- Build trust that outlasts transactions.
- Stay in touch authentically to earn loyalty.
- Convert clients into brand advocates and referral engines.

Chapter 11: The Science of Negotiation – Winning Without Losing

- Master the art of assertive yet compassionate negotiation.
- Handle pricing discussions with grace and control.
- Create win-win deals grounded in integrity.

Chapter 12: The Dharma of Sales – Ethics, Integrity, and Long-Term Success

- Sell with values that honor your customer and your mission.
- Draw inspiration from Yudhishthira and the principles of dharma.
- Build a business and reputation that lasts.

Chapter 13: Understanding Customer Karma – How to Match the Right Product to the Right Person

- Recognize that not every product is for every customer.
- Practice alignment-based selling, guided by purpose and empathy.
- Match needs with value to serve meaningfully.

Chapter 14: The Energy of Money – How to Attract Wealth in Sales

- Shift your mindset from scarcity to abundance.
- Explore spiritual principles of wealth attraction.
- Cultivate the energy that invites prosperity and growth.

Chapter 15: Mastering Follow-Ups – The Lost Art of Persistence

- Learn why most deals are lost in follow-up.
- Use tactful, value-driven strategies to stay top of mind.
- Harness the story of Bhagirath as inspiration for consistent action.

Chapter 16: The Spiritual Psychology of Persuasion – How to Speak to the Subconscious Mind

- Use words and tonality to reach the subconscious mind.
- Learn from ancient practices like mantras and sankalpa.
- Create irresistible messaging rooted in truth and trust.

Chapter 17: Tapasya in Sales – The Power of Perseverance and Self-Discipline

- Discover the deeper meaning of discipline in daily effort.
- Understand how sacrifice and focus build long-term greatness.
- Turn effort into a spiritual path.

Chapter 18: The Inner Game – Mastering the Mind Before the Market

- Win over self-doubt, stress, and emotional turbulence.
- Learn to control your inner world like Arjuna.
- Apply breathwork, intention, and mental mastery to sales.

Chapter 19: Sales Leadership – Becoming a Rainmaker Who Inspires Others

- Make the shift from individual performer to visionary leader.
- Lead with empathy, strength, and strategy.
- Become a mentor who builds a legacy.

Chapter 20: The Ultimate Sales Playbook – Daily Habits for Continuous Growth

- Implement high-performance rituals into your routine.
- Track progress, stay consistent, and evolve constantly.
- Build a lifelong path of mastery, fulfillment, and success.

Preface

From the Author's Heart

"उद्धरेदात्मनाऽत्मानं नात्मानमवसादयेत्।"

("Lift yourself by your own self; do not let yourself fall."
– Bhagavad Gita 6.5)

I didn't set out to write a book. I set out to solve a problem–a very real, very personal one.

I've spent over a decade training sales professionals, leaders, and trainers across the country. I've seen the brightest minds crumble under pressure, the most talented advisors stuck in fear, and good people lose their spark after a few rejections. I've also witnessed ordinary people transform–when they aligned their mindset with the right mission.

Over time, I realized: sales isn't just about targets. It's about transformation.
And transformation begins not in the market–but in the **mind**.

This book is a bridge between **two worlds**–the timeless wisdom of ancient Indian scriptures and the modern-day science of sales mastery. It draws from the **Bhagavad Gita, Ramayana, and the Vedas**, while also anchoring you in practical tools, techniques, and frameworks for consistent success. It is spiritual, but not preachy. Practical, but not shallow.

You'll find strategies, stories, shlokas, and soul in every chapter.

If you're a rookie, this book will prepare you.
If you're a struggler, it will strengthen you.
If you're a leader, it will sharpen and center you.

From Rookie to Rainmaker is more than a title–it's a journey. One that I've lived. One that I've taught. One that I now share with you.

Let's walk it together–with clarity, consistency, and courage.

Ashutosh Pathak
Corporate Trainer | Transformation Coach | MORD-Certified

Overview of the journey ahead

This book is not just about sales strategies. It's about evolving into a complete sales warrior—a Rainmaker who operates with conviction, clarity, and character. You'll learn to combine ancient Indian wisdom with modern sales practices to win not just deals, but also trust, wealth, and purpose. Here's a glimpse of the transformational journey you are about to undertake:

Laying the Foundation: We begin by shaping your inner mindset (**Chapter 1**), defining powerful goals like a warrior (**Chapter 2**), and balancing strategy with emotion through the science of selling (**Chapter 3**).

Mastering the Sales Process: You'll explore the entire journey of a sale—from first contact (**Chapter 4**), finding and qualifying leads (**Chapter 5**), to presenting with influence and storytelling (**Chapters 6 and 7**), and closing deals like a seasoned expert (**Chapter 8**).

Handling Challenges with Wisdom: Learn to overcome objections (**Chapter 9**), build long-term client loyalty (**Chapter 10**), and negotiate with clarity and strength (**Chapter 11**).

Selling with Purpose and Integrity: Dive into the ethical side of sales rooted in dharma (**Chapter 12**), understand how karma affects customer decisions (**Chapter 13**), and explore the energetic power of money and how to attract it (**Chapter 14**).

Sustaining Results Through Discipline: Master the art of effective follow-ups (**Chapter 15**), persuasive communication at a deeper level (**Chapter 16**), and the role of tapasya and discipline in achieving greatness (**Chapter 17**).

Winning the Inner Game: Conquer self-doubt and master your inner world (**Chapter 18**), while evolving into a sales leader who uplifts others (**Chapter 19**).

Living the Rainmaker Life: Wrap it all together with daily rituals, habits, and tools that will make your growth sustainable and joyful (**Chapter 20**).

By the end of this journey, you won't just know how to sell—you'll embody the mindset, discipline, and spiritual depth of a true Rainmaker.

Chapter 1

The Mindset of a Rainmaker

"Your beliefs shape your reality.
If you believe in abundance, you will create it."

The War Before the War

Every salesperson faces two battles–one **outside, in the market**, and another **inside, in the mind**. Before a warrior wins on the battlefield, he must conquer his own doubts, fears, and insecurities.

This is exactly what happened to **Arjuna** in the **Mahabharata**. Standing on the battlefield of **Kurukshetra**, he saw his loved ones on the opposite side and was **paralyzed by self-doubt and fear**. He dropped his bow and said:

"तं तथा कृपया परयाविष्टं अश्रुपूर्णाकुलेक्षणम्।
विषीदन्तमिदं वाक्यमुवाच मधुसूदनः॥"

tam̐ tathā kṛipayāviṣhṭamaśhru pūrṇākulekṣhaṇam
viṣhīdantamidam̐ vākyam uvācha madhusūdanaḥ
(Bhagavad Gita 2.1)

"Overcome with pity, with eyes full of tears and grief-stricken, Arjuna spoke these words to Krishna."

Arjuna had **skills, experience, and resources**, but he was losing the **inner battle of the mind**. This is exactly what happens to salespeople. You may have a great product, training, and leads, but if you lack **mental clarity and conviction**, you will struggle.

So, how do we develop the **mindset of a Rainmaker**–someone who thrives in sales, no matter the situation?

1. The Power of Unwavering Faith

Sales is a field of **uncertainty**. Some days you close big deals; other days, you hear endless **rejections**. What separates an **ordinary salesperson** from a **Rainmaker** is **faith in oneself and the process.**

Krishna tells Arjuna:

"न हि कश्चित्क्षणमपि जातु तिष्ठत्यकर्मकृत्।
कार्यते ह्यवशः कर्म सर्वः प्रकृतिजैर्गुणैः॥"

na hi kaśhchit kṣhaṇam api jātu tiṣhṭhatyakarma-kṛit
kāryate hyavaśhaḥ karma sarvaḥ prakṛiti-jair guṇaiḥ
(Bhagavad Gita 3.5)

"No one can remain inactive even for a moment. Everyone is forced to act according to the qualities born of nature."

A Rainmaker accepts rejection as part of the journey and keeps moving. They believe in Karma Yoga–continuous action without attachment to results.

2. Handling Rejection Like a Warrior

A struggling salesperson takes rejection **personally**. A Rainmaker sees it as **feedback.**

Ravana's greatest mistake in the Ramayana was that he never **accepted his flaws**. Even when **Mandodari (his wife) and Vibhishana (his brother) warned him** that kidnapping Sita would bring his downfall, he ignored them. He was so **attached to his ego** that he couldn't see his mistakes.

But a Rainmaker listens, learns, and adapts. Krishna says:

"यं हि न व्यथयन्त्येते पुरुषं पुरुषर्षभ |
समदुःखसुखं धीरं सोऽमृतत्वाय कल्पते ||

yaṁ hi na vyathayantyete puruṣhaṁ puruṣharṣhabha
sama-duḥkha-sukhaṁ dhīraṁ so 'mṛitatvāya kalpate
(Bhagavad Gita 2.15)

"That person who is steady in pleasure and pain, who remains unshaken, is fit for immortality."

Next time a prospect says **"I'm not interested,"** don't see it as rejection—see it as an opportunity to learn.

3. The Art of Conviction: Speak with Power

Why do some salespeople **convince effortlessly**, while others struggle?

The answer lies in **conviction**. If you don't **fully believe** in your product, your prospect won't either.

Hanuman is the **greatest example of conviction.** When he was sent to find Sita, he had no **map or exact location**, yet he told himself:

"There is no doubt. I will find Mother Sita, or I will destroy Lanka itself!"

This is the attitude of a Rainmaker. When you walk into a sales pitch, tell yourself:

"I will close this deal today, or I will at least leave an unforgettable impression!"

Krishna reinforces this mindset:

"श्रद्धावान् लभते ज्ञानं तत्परः संयतेन्द्रियः।
ज्ञानं लब्ध्वा परां शान्तिमचिरेणाधिगच्छति॥"

śhraddhāvānllabhate jñānaṁ tat-paraḥ sanyatendriyaḥ
jñānaṁ labdhvā parāṁ śhāntim achireṇādhigachchhati
(Bhagavad Gita 4.39)

"A person with faith, who is dedicated and has control over his senses, attains wisdom. Having gained wisdom, he soon attains supreme peace."

A Rainmaker believes in their own words, their product, and their mission. And because of this, customers trust them.

4. Discipline and Daily Actions: The Kaizen Principle

The **biggest mistake** salespeople make? Inconsistency. They work hard for **one week**, then relax for **two weeks**.

Krishna warns:

"सत्त्वानुरूपा सर्वस्य श्रद्धा भवति भारत।
श्रद्धामयोऽयं पुरुषो यो यच्छ्रद्धः स एव सः॥"

sattvānurūpā sarvasya śhraddhā bhavati bhārata
śhraddhā-mayo 'yaṁ puruṣho yo yach-chhraddhaḥ sa eva saḥ
(Bhagavad Gita 17.3)

"A person is made of their faith. Whatever a person believes in, that is what they become."

The Japanese call this the **Kaizen Principle**—small daily improvements lead to massive success over time. A Rainmaker **follows a disciplined daily routine**:

- **Prospecting daily** (Finding new leads)
- **Pitching daily** (Making calls and meetings)
- **Follow-ups daily** (Staying in touch with clients)

Even **one hour of consistent sales effort daily** compounds into massive success over months and years.

5. Overcoming Fear of Pricing: The Law of Value

Many salespeople hesitate to quote **high prices** for their products. They fear losing the deal. But Rainmakers **never hesitate** because they **understand value.**

Krishna says:

"यद्यदाचरति श्रेष्ठस्तत्तदेवेतरो जनः।
स यत्प्रमाणं कुरुते लोकस्तदनुवर्तते॥"

yad yad ācharati śhreṣhṭhas tat tad evetaro janaḥ
sa yat pramāṇaṁ kurute lokas tad anuvartate
(Bhagavad Gita 3.21)

"People follow the standards set by great individuals. Whatever they do, others will follow."

If **you hesitate** while quoting the price, the customer will **hesitate to buy**. But if you speak with **conviction**, the customer will **see the value and pay.**

Rainmakers believe in their worth. They never discount themselves.

Conclusion: Think Like a Rainmaker

A Rainmaker controls their mind, believes in their product, and takes action daily.

Sales is not just about techniques—it is about inner mastery. The Bhagavad Gita teaches us that our greatest enemy is doubt, and our greatest weapon is belief.

So, next time you feel discouraged, remember Krishna's words:

"मन्मना भव मद्भक्तो मद्याजी मां नमस्कुरु।
मामेवैष्यसि सत्यं ते प्रतिजाने प्रियोऽसि मे॥"

man-manā bhava mad-bhakto mad-yājī māṁ namaskuru
mām evaiṣhyasi satyaṁ te pratijāne priyo 'si me
(Bhagavad Gita 18.65)

"Fix your mind on me, be devoted to me, worship me, and surrender to me. I promise you shall come to me, for you are dear to me."

If you truly dedicate yourself to your sales journey with **faith, discipline, and conviction**, you will not just succeed—**you will become a Rainmaker.**

Chapter 2:

Lakshya – The Art of Goal Setting, the Warrior Way

"When your vision is clear, distractions disappear."

Introduction: What Is Lakshya?

The word **Lakshya** means target, goal, or aim. In the world of sales, your Lakshya is your sales target, your income goal, your dream destination. But it is more than a number. It is the reason you wake up with energy. It gives your actions direction. Just like an archer without a target cannot hit anything, a salesperson without a goal will feel lost and tired.

Ancient Indian wisdom teaches us not just to set goals—but to **pursue them like warriors**. Arjuna, the hero of the Mahabharata, showed us how to aim, focus, and act without attachment.

Let's learn the art of goal setting from our scriptures and blend it with practical sales strategies.

The Arjuna Mindset – See Only the Eye of the Bird

Once, Guru Dronacharya wanted to test his students. He placed a wooden bird on a tree and asked each of them to aim at its eye.

He asked Yudhishthira, "What do you see?"

Yudhishthira said, "I see the bird, the tree, and the branch."

Drona said, "Step back."

He asked Arjuna, "What do you see?"

Arjuna replied, "I see only the eye of the bird."

Drona smiled and said, "Shoot."

This is the **Lakshya mindset**—complete focus on your goal. When you are clear about your sales target, you will stop being distracted by fear, comparison, or rejection.

Real-Life Example: Rajesh, a salesperson, used to get distracted by daily pressure. But when he created a clear vision—to earn ₹10 lakhs this year, help his family buy a home, and qualify for a foreign trip—he became more focused. He stopped gossiping in the office, avoided negative colleagues, and hit his targets month after month.

Lesson: Clarity of Lakshya creates energy and filters distractions.

Shrimad Bhagavad Gita on Goal and Action

One of the most powerful shlokas on goal setting and action is:

"कर्मण्येवाधिकारस्ते मा फलेषु कदाचन।
मा कर्मफलहेतुर्भूर्मा ते संगोऽस्त्वकर्मणि॥"

karmaṇy-evādhikāras te mā phaleṣhu kadāchana
mā karma-phala-hetur bhūr mā te saṅgo 'stv akarmaṇi
(Bhagavad Gita 2.47)

"You have the right to perform your duty, but not to the fruits of your actions. Do not let the results be your motivation, and do not become attached to inaction."

This is the spiritual foundation of high performance. Work with full intensity. Be loyal to effort, not outcome. The result will take care of itself.

Sales Application: Don't stress about closing every deal. Make the call. Give your best pitch. Follow up sincerely. But stay detached from the result. If a client says "no," don't feel bad. Keep moving.

Another gem from the Gita:

"योगस्थः कुरु कर्माणि सङ्गं त्यक्त्वा धनञ्जय।
सिद्ध्यसिद्ध्योः समो भूत्वा समत्वं योग उच्यते॥"

yogasthaḥ kuru karmāṇi saṅgaṁ tyaktvā dhanañjaya
siddhy-asiddhyoḥ samo bhūtvā samatvaṁ yoga uchyate
(Bhagavad Gita 2.48)

"Perform your actions established in yoga, O Arjuna, abandoning attachment and remaining balanced in success and failure. Such equanimity is called yoga."

Ramayana – Lord Rama's Clarity of Purpose

In the Ramayana, Lord Rama had one clear purpose: to rescue Sita and destroy evil. No matter how many obstacles came—crossing rivers, facing demons, losing allies—he never lost sight of his Lakshya.

When Ravana kidnapped Sita, Rama didn't sit and cry. He took action. He built alliances, formed a team (like a sales team!), planned his path, and fought with full focus.

Quote from Ramcharitmanas:

"रघुकुल रीति सदा चलि आई। प्राण जाए पर वचन न जाई॥"

"The rule of the Raghu clan has always been: One may lose their life, but never their word."

Lesson for Salespeople: Once you set a goal, stay committed. Don't change it because things get tough. Be like Rama–faithful to your mission.

The Power of Sankalpa – Intent Drives Action

In ancient Vedic practices, everything begins with a **Sankalpa**–a sacred intention.

Before a yajna (ritual), the priest declares: "I take this Sankalpa to do..."

Salespeople should begin every day with a Sankalpa:

- "Today, I will make 10 meaningful calls."
- "This week, I will close 3 new clients."

Your brain follows your intent. When your Sankalpa is clear, your actions become purposeful.

Practical Tip: Write your daily goal on paper. Speak it aloud. This activates the subconscious mind.

Scriptural Reference:

"संकल्पमूलं धर्मस्य" –

Dharma begins with Sankalpa. ***(Smriti Granthas)***

If your goal is strong, your path will open. If your goal is weak, your energy will be scattered.

Designing a Warrior's Goal Plan

Let's now build a goal-setting system inspired by warriors:

Step 1: Define your target (Lakshya)
Be specific. Not "I want to earn more" but "I will close ₹10 lakhs in Q1."

Step 2: Understand your WHY
Why do you want to hit this goal? For your child's education? For a family trip? A deeper purpose keeps you motivated.

Step 3: Break it into small goals

- Daily calls: 10
- Weekly meetings: 5
- Monthly conversions: 8 clients

Step 4: Create a daily ritual

- Morning Sankalpa
- 3 powerful affirmations
- Evening review

Step 5: Detach from results
Like Krishna said, stay loyal to the process. Results will follow.

Step 6: Celebrate progress

Even small wins should be celebrated. This keeps motivation high.

Ancient Wisdom for Modern Sales Goals

Let's gather key shlokas and wisdom:

Bhagavad Gita 6.5

"उद्धरेदात्मनाऽत्मानं नात्मानमवसादयेत्।"

"Elevate yourself by your own efforts; do not degrade yourself."

Vishnu Purana

"धैर्यं सर्वसंपदाम् मूलम्।"

"Courage is the root of all success."

Chanakya Niti

"संकटे ये न मुञ्चन्ति ते बान्धवाः।"

"Those who stand by you in crisis are your true allies."

Mundaka Upanishad

"सत्येन लभ्यस्तपसा ह्येष आत्मा।"

"The Self is attained by truth, discipline, and deep desire."

Conclusion: Be the Arjuna of Sales

Arjuna did not fear the battlefield because he had focus, purpose, and the right guide (Krishna). In the same way, every salesperson can become a Rainmaker if they:

- Set a clear Lakshya
- Act daily with discipline
- Detach from results
- Stay inspired by ancient wisdom

Whenever you feel lost, read this:

"योगस्थः कुरु कर्माणि सङ्गं त्यक्त्वा धनञ्जय।"

Stay rooted in your goal. Keep acting. And like Arjuna, you too will hit the bullseye.

Assignments

- Write down your Top 3 goals for this quarter.
- Break them into daily actions.
- Create a Sankalpa for each morning and repeat it aloud.

You are a warrior. Your Lakshya awaits. Aim. Focus. Fire.

Chapter 3

The Art and Science of Sales – Balancing Emotion and Strategy for Maximum Success

Introduction: The Two Sides of Sales

Sales is often seen as a battlefield–one where strategy, logic, and precision (science) must work in harmony with creativity, persuasion, and human connection (art). The best sales professionals, the true Rainmakers, are those who master this delicate balance.

Just as **Lord Krishna in the Bhagavad Gita** guided Arjuna with both **logical reasoning** (**Jnana Yoga**) and **emotional wisdom** (**Bhakti Yoga**), a great salesperson must blend **science** (**data, techniques, process**) and **art** (**relationship-building, storytelling, intuition**) to create success.

Why Sales Requires Both Creativity and Structure

A purely mechanical, robotic approach to sales will fail because humans buy based on emotions and justify with logic. On the other hand, a purely emotional, relationship-driven approach without a structured process will lead to inconsistency.

The **science** of sales includes:

- ☑ Understanding customer psychology
- ☑ Implementing structured sales processes
- ☑ Using data-driven decision-making
- ☑ Following a disciplined routine and tracking performance

The **art** of sales includes:

- ☑ Building deep emotional connections with clients
- ☑ Storytelling and persuasion
- ☑ Adapting to different personalities and sales scenarios
- ☑ Using creativity to solve problems and handle objections

When to Rely on Intuition vs. Data-Driven Decision-Making

Sales leaders often ask: Should I trust my gut or the numbers?

The answer is: **Both.** The key is to know **when** to use logic and when to trust intuition.

▶ Data should guide your prospecting, pipeline management, and strategic decisions.

▶ Intuition helps in real-time interactions, negotiations, and relationship-building.

In the Mahabharata, **Lord Krishna demonstrates both logic and intuition**. When Duryodhana refused to give the Pandavas even five villages, Krishna did not waste time in further negotiation (logic). But when Arjuna hesitated on the battlefield, Krishna appealed to his emotions and sense of duty (intuition).

श्रीभगवानुवाच |

अशोच्यानन्वशोचस्त्वं प्रज्ञावादांश्च भाषसे |
गतासूनगतासूंश्च नानुशोचन्ति पण्डिताः ||

aśhochyān-anvaśhochas-tvaṁ prajñā-vādānśh cha bhāṣhase
gatāsūn-agatāsūnśh-cha nānuśhochanti paṇḍitāḥ
(Bhagavad Gita 2.11)

"The Supreme Lord said: You grieve for those who should not be grieved for, yet speak words of wisdom. The wise do not mourn for the living or the dead."

This shloka reminds us that overthinking and emotional distress cloud judgment. A true Rainmaker, like a warrior, must **act with clarity**—combining wisdom (science) and courage (art).

How Ancient Wisdom Balances Logic and Emotion in Sales

In **Chanakya Neeti**, Chanakya states:

"साधूनामपि दुर्जनः शिक्षामादत्ते।"

sadhunamapi durjanah shikshaamadatte

"Even a virtuous person can learn from an unethical one."

This means a salesperson should learn from both logical thinkers (scientists, analysts) and great orators (storytellers, leaders) to master both aspects of sales.

Similarly, in the Ramayana, Lord Hanuman used logic and strategy when searching for Sita Mata but relied on emotion and persuasion when delivering Lord Rama's message to her.

This shows that both science (strategy, planning, execution) and art (persuasion, emotional intelligence, adaptability) are essential in any mission—including sales.

Case Studies of Top Sales Performers Who Master Both Aspects

Case Study 1: Steve Jobs – The Artist and Scientist in Sales

Steve Jobs was a master of blending **data-driven strategy** (science) with **persuasive storytelling** (art).

▶ He used market research and user behavior insights to create revolutionary products. (Science)

▶ His product launches were emotional experiences, making people feel connected to Apple. (Art)

He knew that numbers alone don't sell, but emotions backed by logic do.

Case Study 2: Warren Buffett – The Logical Seller with an Emotional Touch

Warren Buffett, one of the greatest investors, sells the idea of long-term investing using both data and storytelling.

▶ He uses **financial metrics and economic principles** to justify his investment choices. (Science)

▶ He shares **engaging, relatable stories** in his annual letters to inspire trust. (Art)

Becoming a Balanced Sales Warrior: Actionable Steps

✅ **Master the Science:** Learn sales psychology, negotiation techniques, and data-driven strategies.

✅ **Embrace the Art:** Develop emotional intelligence, storytelling skills, and deep client relationships.

✅ **Know When to Switch:** Use logic for planning, but intuition for real-time decision-making.

✅ **Learn from Ancient Wisdom:** Study figures like Krishna, Hanuman, and Chanakya for lessons in balance.

Final Thought: A True Rainmaker is Both a Scientist and an Artist

A warrior does not go into battle with just a sword or just a shield—**he carries both.** Likewise, a great salesperson must **combine strategy with creativity, logic with persuasion, data with intuition.**

As Krishna tells Arjuna:

योगस्थः कुरु कर्माणि संगं त्यक्त्वा धनंजय |
सिद्ध्यसिद्ध्योः समो भूत्वा समत्वं योग उच्यते ||

yoga-sthaḥ kuru karmāṇi saṅgaṁ tyaktvā dhanañjaya
siddhy-asiddhyoḥ samo bhūtvā samatvaṁ yoga uchyate
(Bhagavad Gita 2.48)

"Perform your duty, O Arjuna, with equanimity, abandoning attachment to success and failure. Such balance in action is called yoga."

A **Rainmaker** does not just chase targets—he **masters the art and science of sales**, knowing that true success lies in **balance**.

Chapter 4

Mastering the Sales Process—From First Contact to Closing the Deal

"Sales is not about pushing a product;
it's about guiding a prospect to the right decision."

The Game of Chess and Sales

Imagine you're playing a **game of chess**. A rookie moves pieces **randomly**, hoping to win. But a grandmaster has a **strategy**–every move is **calculated** to reach a checkmate.

Sales are the same. Amateurs wing it. Rainmakers follow a process.

In this chapter, we break down **the entire sales process**—step by step—so that you move from being a **rookie salesperson** to a **sales grandmaster.**

1. The First Move: Making an Impactful First Contact

"The first impression is not the last impression–it's the beginning of trust."

Most salespeople fail **in the first 30 seconds** of interaction. Why? Because they focus on **selling** instead of **connecting**.

Real-Life Case Study: The Power of Connection

A financial advisor once struggled to sell high-ticket insurance policies. He focused on explaining **features and returns but** failed to build trust.

One day, he changed his approach. Instead of pitching immediately, he asked, "**What is the one thing you want to secure for your family's future?**"

The prospect opened up about his **dream to send his daughter abroad for education**. The advisor then aligned the insurance solution with this dream. Result? **A ₹25 lakh policy sold in 30 minutes.**

Bhagavad Gita Insight: The Art of Winning Trust

Krishna built **trust with Arjuna** before guiding him. Instead of **giving direct commands**, he first addressed Arjuna's emotions:

तमुवाच हृषीकेशः प्रहसन्निव भारत |
सेनयोरुभयोर्मध्ये विषीदन्तमिदं वचः || 2.10||

tam-uvācha hṛiṣhīkeśhaḥ prahasanniva bhārata
senayorubhayor-madhye viṣhīdantam-idaṁ vachaḥ
(Bhagavad Gita 2.10)

"Krishna, smiling as if in amusement, spoke to Arjuna with compassion."

A Rainmaker knows:

- People buy from those they trust.
- First connect, then sell.

2. The Discovery Phase: Uncovering the Prospect's True Need

Most salespeople make the mistake of **assuming** what the customer needs. A Rainmaker **asks and listens.**

Real-Life Scenario: The Power of Deep Listening

A salesperson selling mutual funds once asked a client, "Why are you hesitant about investing?" The client said, "I don't understand how markets work."

Instead of pushing products, the salesperson spent 20 minutes educating the client on mutual funds in simple terms. The client felt comfortable and invested ₹5 lakhs on the spot.

Bhagavad Gita Wisdom: Listening Before Advising

Krishna **listened to Arjuna's dilemma** before giving him advice. He let Arjuna express **his fears and doubts** before responding.

"तं तथा कृपयाविष्टमश्रुपूर्णाकुलेक्षणम् ।
विषीदन्तमिदं वाक्यमुवाच मधुसूदनः ॥"

taṁ tathā kṛipayāviṣhṭamaśhru pūrṇākulekṣhaṇam
viṣhīdantamidaṁ vākyam uvācha madhusūdanaḥ
(Bhagavad Gita 2.1)

"Seeing Arjuna overwhelmed with pity and sadness, Krishna then spoke to him."

A Rainmaker doesn't force a product—they uncover a need and solve a problem.

3. The Art of Presenting: Selling the Outcome, Not the Product

Customers **don't buy products**. They buy **outcomes**–solutions to their pain points.

Example: The Wrong vs. Right Way to Present a Product
Imagine you're selling a health insurance policy.

- **Rookie Pitch:** "Our policy covers ₹10 lakh, includes hospitalization, and offers tax benefits."
- **Rainmaker Pitch:** "This policy ensures that even if an unexpected medical emergency happens, your family's finances remain untouched. It's not just insurance; it's peace of mind."

Bhagavad Gita Insight: Focus on the End Goal

Krishna didn't just tell Arjuna to fight; he **showed him the bigger picture**–his duty as a warrior, dharma, and ultimate purpose.

"कर्मण्येवाधिकारस्ते मा फलेषु कदाचन।"

karmaṇy-evādhikāras te mā phaleṣhu kadāchana
(Bhagavad Gita 2.47)

"You have control over your actions, but not over the results."

A Rainmaker focuses on the **solution**, not just the **features.**

4. Handling Objections: The Art of Overcoming Resistance

Customers will always have objections–**price, trust, need, or urgency.** Instead of fearing them, Rainmakers **prepare for them.**

Real-Life Case Study: Overcoming the Price Objection

A luxury car salesman once had a customer say, **"I love the car, but it's too expensive."**

Instead of dropping the price, he asked: **"Compared to what?"**

The customer realized he was comparing the car to **a cheaper model with fewer features**. The salesman then highlighted the **value—safety, comfort, and long-term prestige.** The customer bought the car **without a discount.**

Bhagavad Gita Wisdom: Conquering Doubts with Logic

Arjuna had doubts about fighting, and Krishna answered with **logic and wisdom.**

"न हि ज्ञानेन सदृशं पवित्रमिह विद्यते।"

na hi jñānena sadṛiśhaṁ pavitramiha vidyate
(Bhagavad Gita 4.38)

"There is nothing as purifying as knowledge in this world."

A Rainmaker doesn't argue with objections—they educate and reframe.

5. Closing the Deal: Sealing the Victory

The biggest mistake salespeople make? Not asking for the sale. A Rainmaker guides the customer to a confident YES.

Real-Life Example: The Power of the Right Close

A real estate agent once struggled to close deals because he kept saying, **"Would you like to think about it?"**

One day, he changed his approach and asked, "When do you want to move into your new home?"

By assuming the sale was happening, he made it easier for customers to say YES. His closing rate doubled.

Bhagavad Gita Wisdom: Decision and Action

Krishna didn't just give Arjuna **knowledge**—he made him take **action.**

हतो वा प्राप्स्यसि स्वर्गं जित्वा वा भोक्ष्यसे महीम् |
तस्मादुत्तिष्ठ कौन्तेय युद्धाय कृतनिश्चय: ||

hato vā prāpsyasi swargaṁ jitvā vā bhokṣhyase mahīm
tasmād uttiṣhṭha kaunteya yuddhāya kṛita-niśhchayaḥ
(Bhagavad Gita 2.37)

"Therefore, stand up with determination and fight!"

A Rainmaker **doesn't hesitate**—they lead the customer to **decision and action.**

Conclusion: The Sales Process of a Rainmaker

A **Rookie salesperson** talks, hopes, and waits.

A **Rainmaker** follows a structured process:

1. **First Contact** - Build trust before selling.
2. **Discovery** - Uncover needs, don't assume.
3. **Presentation** - Sell solutions, not products.
4. **Objection Handling** - Educate, don't argue.
5. **Closing** - Lead the customer to a YES.

By mastering these **five steps**, you don't just become a better salesperson—**you become unstoppable.**

Chapter 5

The Art of Prospecting – How to Find and Attract High-Quality Leads

"He who waits for opportunities may get some,
but he who creates opportunities becomes unstoppable."

Introduction: The Salesperson's Biggest Challenge

Imagine walking into your office every morning, staring at your empty calendar, and thinking—where do I find my next customer?

This is the biggest challenge in sales: Without leads, there are no sales. Without sales, there's no business.

Many salespeople spend their days reaching out to random people, hoping for a sale. They attend meetings that lead nowhere. They call prospects who aren't interested. They push products on people who don't need them.

A Rainmaker, however, plays the game differently. They don't waste time on weak leads. They don't try to sell to everyone. They focus on high-quality prospects—people who need, can afford, and have the authority to buy.

Before the great Kurukshetra war, Arjuna didn't just pick any warriors for his side. He sought powerful allies—Lord Krishna, Bheema, Yudhishthira, and Nakula. He knew that choosing the right people would determine the outcome of the war.

Sales is no different.

A Rainmaker builds a strong pipeline by targeting the right prospects—because the right effort in the right direction leads to victory.

Bhagavad Gita Insight: The Right Effort in the Right Direction

Krishna tells Arjuna:

"युक्ताहारविहारस्य युक्तचेष्टस्य कर्मसु ।
युक्तस्वप्नावबोधस्य योगो भवति दुःखहा ॥"

yuktāhāra-vihārasya yukta-cheṣhṭasya karmasu
yukta-svapnāvabodhasya yogo bhavati duḥkha-hā
(Bhagavad Gita 6.17)

"One who is balanced in effort, actions, rest, and awareness achieves success."

A Rainmaker doesn't chase everyone—they focus on the right people.

1. The Mistake Most Salespeople Make in Prospecting

Most salespeople make one deadly mistake—they treat everyone as a potential buyer.

Real-Life Case Study: The Insurance Agent Who Changed His Approach

An insurance agent in Mumbai was struggling. He met 100 people every week but closed only one or two policies.

One day, his mentor told him:

"Stop selling to everyone. Sell only to people who need it."

He changed his approach. Instead of meeting random people, he identified two high-potential groups:

1. Business owners who needed insurance for tax-saving.
2. Young fathers who wanted financial security for their families.

What happened?

✅ He reduced meetings to 30 per week.

✅ He started closing 10+ policies per week.

Lesson?

A Rookie talks to everyone.

A Rainmaker talks to qualified buyers.

2. The Three Golden Filters: Identifying the Right Prospects

A great prospect is someone who:

✔ Needs the Product (Do they have a genuine need?)

✔ Has the Ability to Pay (Can they afford it?)

✔ Has the Authority to Decide (Are they the decision-maker?)

If any of these three are missing, you are wasting time.

Mahabharata Wisdom: Duryodhana's Wrong Allies vs. Krishna's Right Strategy

Duryodhana filled his army with low-quality soldiers–greedy kings who were fighting for money. Krishna, on the other hand, told Arjuna:

कर्मणो ह्यपि बोद्धव्यं बोद्धव्यं च विकर्मण: |
अकर्मणश्च बोद्धव्यं गहना कर्मणो गति: ||

karmaṇo hyapi boddhavyaṁ boddhavyaṁ cha vikarmaṇaḥ
akarmaṇaśh cha boddhavyaṁ gahanā karmaṇo gatiḥ
(Bhagavad Gita 4.17)

"One must understand what is right action, wrong action, and inaction."

Arjuna chose warriors who were aligned with his mission–and won.

Salespeople should do the same–filter out bad prospects and focus on the right ones.

3. Where to Find the Best Prospects

Many salespeople struggle because they don't know where to look.

Here's where Rainmakers find high-quality leads:

✔ Existing Clients - Ask them for referrals.

✔ Networking Events - Meet decision-makers directly.

✔ Social Media (LinkedIn, Instagram, Facebook Groups) - Engage with potential buyers.

✔ Community & Religious Gatherings - Many people make financial decisions here.

✔ Workshops & Seminars – Educate first, sell later.

Real-Life Scenario: The Power of Networking

A mutual fund distributor once attended a Rotary Club meeting where HNIs (High Net Worth Individuals) were present.

He gave a small talk on wealth creation.

At the end, 5 businessmen approached him–and he closed ₹50 lakh in investments.

Lesson?

A Rookie waits for clients.

A Rainmaker creates opportunities.

4. The Approach: Making the First Move Without Sounding Salesy

Prospecting is not about hard selling. It's about building curiosity and trust.

Ramayana Insight: How Hanuman Approached Sita in Lanka

When Hanuman reached Lanka, he didn't shout or directly tell Sita to trust him.

Instead, he first:

✔ Gained her confidence by reciting Lord Rama's story.

✔ Showed proof (Rama's ring) to establish credibility.

✔ Slowly built trust before revealing his real purpose.

Salespeople should do the same:

✔ Warm Up the Prospect – Start with a friendly conversation.

✔ Ask the Right Questions - *"What's your biggest challenge?"*

✔ Create Curiosity - *"What if I could show you a solution in 5 minutes?"*

✔ Give Proof - Share testimonials and case studies.

✔ Close with Confidence - *"Would you like to see how this can help you?"*

5. Assignment: Your Personal Prospecting Plan

Let's put knowledge into action.

Your Task:

☑ Make a List of 50 Potential Prospects

☑ Identify at least 10 high-quality leads.

☑ Choose Your Prospecting Channel: Where will you find them? (Existing clients, social media, referrals, networking?)

☑ Craft Your Opening Script: What will be your first sentence?

☑ Set a Goal: How many prospects will you reach this week?

Conclusion: Prospecting Like a Rainmaker

A Rookie chases everyone.

A Rainmaker attracts and converts the right people.

By mastering prospecting, you'll never run out of leads—and sales will feel effortless.

Chapter 6

The Psychology of Selling – How to Influence and Persuade Anyone

"The secret of sales is not in what you sell,
but in how you make people feel about buying it."

The Battlefield of the Mind: Why Selling is an Art of Influence

During the Kurukshetra war, Krishna never lifted a weapon, yet he was the most powerful force on the battlefield. Why?

Because he influenced and persuaded Arjuna using clarity, logic, emotions, and authority.

Selling is no different. Sales is not about convincing people–it's about guiding them to realize what's best for them.

Bhagavad Gita Insight: Mastering the Mind to Master Sales

Krishna tells Arjuna:

उद्धरेदात्मनात्मानं नात्मानमवसादयेत् |
आत्मैव ह्यात्मनो बन्धुरात्मैव रिपुरात्मनः ||

uddhared ātmanātmānaṁ nātmānam avasādayet
ātmaiva hyātmano bandhur ātmaiva ripur ātmanaḥ
(Bhagavad Gita 6.5)

"A person must elevate himself through his own mind; never degrade himself. The mind is a friend to one who controls it and an enemy to one who doesn't."

In sales, your mindset determines your influence. Control your thoughts, and you control the customer's decision-making.

1. The Science of Persuasion: How the Human Mind Makes Decisions

People don't buy logically—they buy emotionally and justify it with logic later.

Mahabharata Example: Krishna's Persuasion Before War

Before the war, Krishna went to Hastinapura to negotiate peace. Instead of arguing, he used three psychological triggers:

✔ Reciprocity – He reminded the Kauravas of past goodwill.

✔ Authority – He spoke with divine wisdom.

✔ Social Proof – He showed that most kings supported the Pandavas.

But Duryodhana resisted—because he was blinded by ego.

In sales, you'll meet two types of buyers:

✔ Logical buyers – Need facts, proof, guarantees.

✔ Emotional buyers – Need stories, emotions, trust.

A Rainmaker understands both.

2. The Five Pillars of Persuasion: Krishna's Sales Masterclass

Sales is the art of leading the customer's mind toward a "Yes."

1. Trust: Without Trust, There is No Sale

People buy from those they like and trust.

NLP Technique: Mirroring & Matching

✔ Subtly mirror body language, tone, and speech patterns of the customer to create an instant subconscious connection.

✔ Krishna did this effortlessly–adjusting his approach based on who he was speaking to (Arjuna vs. Duryodhana).

Real-Life Scenario: The Doctor Who Increased Sales Without Selling

A financial advisor noticed that doctors trusted medical representatives more than insurance agents.

So, he started offering free financial seminars for doctors–without selling anything. After six months, doctors trusted him and willingly bought insurance from him.

Lesson: Build trust first, sales will follow.

2. Authority: Be the Expert

A buyer will always listen to an expert over a salesperson.

Ramayana Example: Why Rama's Word Was Irresistible
When Lord Rama asked the Vanaras (monkey army) to build a bridge to Lanka, no one questioned him. Why?

Because he was their trusted leader.

✔ NLP Technique: Anchoring

Salespeople can create a positive buying experience by associating their product with certainty, trust, and authority (like Krishna did for Arjuna).

Sales Tip: Use testimonials, credentials, and success stories to establish authority.

3. Scarcity: What is Rare Becomes Valuable

People want what they can't easily have.

Krishna says:

न हि कश्चित्क्षणमपि जातु तिष्ठत्यकर्मकृत् |
कार्यते ह्यवशः कर्म सर्वः प्रकृतिजैर्गुणैः || 5||

na hi kaśhchit kṣhaṇam api jātu tiṣhṭhatyakarma-kṛit
kāryate hyavaśhaḥ karma sarvaḥ prakṛiti-jair guṇaiḥ
(Bhagavad Gita 3.5)

"No one can remain inactive even for a moment; everyone is compelled to act by the forces of nature."

✔ NLP Technique: Future Pacing

Describe a future where the prospect doesn't act—let them mentally experience the cost of inaction.

Example: Instead of saying "Buy anytime," say "This offer expires in 3 days."

4. Emotional Connection: People Buy Feelings, Not Products

Logic opens the mind, but emotions move the heart.

✔ NLP Technique: Sensory Language & Visualization

Use words that help the customer see, feel, and experience the benefits before purchasing.

Mahabharata Example: Karna's Emotional Loyalty
Duryodhana won over Karna's loyalty not by money—but by giving him emotional validation.

Sales Tip: Use personal stories, case studies, and empathy to create emotional bonds.

5. The Power of Silence: Let the Customer Convince Themselves

Many salespeople talk too much and lose the sale.

Ramayana Insight: The Silent Wisdom of Hanuman
When Hanuman met Sita in Lanka, he waited before speaking. He let her observe him, analyze him, and feel safe.

✔ NLP Technique: Embedded Commands & The Pause

Ask a strong question. Then stay silent.

✔ The first one to break the silence... loses the sale.

3. How to Handle Objections Like Krishna in Kurukshetra

Objections are not rejections—they are hidden buying signals.

Krishna tells Arjuna:

तस्मादज्ञानसम्भूतं हृत्स्थं ज्ञानासिनात्मनः |
छित्त्वैनं संशयं योगमातिष्ठोत्तिष्ठ भारत || 42||

tasmād ajñāna-sambhūtaṁ hṛit-sthaṁ jñānāsinātmanaḥ
chhittvainaṁ sanśhayaṁ yogam ātiṣhṭhottiṣhṭha bhārata
(Bhagavad Gita 4.42)

"Destroy doubts with the sword of wisdom. Take action!"

✔ NLP Technique: Reframing Objections

Turn objections into motivations by shifting perspectives.

Example:

✖ "It's too expensive."

✔ "Compared to what? What's more expensive–this solution or the problem staying unsolved?"

4. Assignment: Persuasion in Action

Let's turn knowledge into real results.

Your Task:

✔ Identify a Stubborn Prospect - Someone who hasn't said "Yes" yet.

✔ Choose a Persuasion Strategy:

- Build trust?
- Use scarcity?
- Tell an emotional story?

✔ Apply It This Week - See if it changes the response.

Conclusion: Sell Like Krishna, Win Like Arjuna

✔ A Rookie argues.

✔ A Rainmaker influences.

By mastering NLP techniques, psychology, and persuasion, you'll turn no's into yes effortlessly.

Chapter 7

The Power of Storytelling in Sales – How to Win Hearts and Close Deals

The Art of Storytelling: Why It Works in Sales

Humans are wired for stories. Since ancient times, wisdom and values have been passed down through storytelling–whether in the form of the Vedic scriptures, the grand narratives of the *Ramayana* and *Mahabharata*, or the insightful parables of sages.

Sales, at its core, is about connection. And storytelling is the most powerful way to forge that connection. A well-told story engages emotions, simplifies complex ideas, and makes a pitch memorable. Neuroscientific research shows that stories activate multiple areas of the brain, making them more persuasive than mere data or logic.

Even **Lord Krishna used storytelling to transform Arjuna's mindset** in the *Bhagavad Gita*, rather than merely instructing him.

न बुद्धिभेदं जनयेदज्ञानां कर्मसङ्गिनाम् |
जोषयेत्सर्वकर्माणि विद्वान्युक्तः समाचरन् ||

na buddhi-bhedaṁ janayed ajñānāṁ karma-saṅginām
joṣayet sarva-karmāṇi vidvān yuktaḥ samācharan
Bhagavad Gita - Chapter 3, Verse 26

"The wise should not unsettle the ignorant who are attached to action. Instead, they should inspire them by performing all actions in a spirit of devotion."

A great salesperson follows this wisdom. Rather than overwhelming customers with facts, they **use stories to guide them** toward the right decision.

How Lord Krishna Used Storytelling to Persuade Arjuna

On the battlefield of Kurukshetra, Arjuna was paralyzed by doubt. Instead of commanding him, Krishna used:

☑ **Relatable metaphors** - Comparing the body to worn-out clothes that the soul discards.

वासांसि जीर्णानि यथा विहाय
नवानि गृह्णाति नरोऽपराणि ।
तथा शरीराणि विहाय जीर्णा
न्यन्यानि संयाति नवानि देही ॥

vāsāṁsi jīrṇāni yathā vihāya
navāni gṛhṇāti naro'parāṇi
tathā śarīrāṇi vihāya jīrṇā
nyāni sanyāti navāni dehī
Bhagavad Gita - Chapter 2, Verse 22

"Just as a person discards old garments and wears new ones, the soul discards an old body and enters a new one."

A great sales story follows this pattern—helping customers discard **old limiting beliefs** and embrace **new possibilities**.

✅ **Historical references** – Reminding Arjuna of past warriors who upheld their duty.

✅ **Emotional impact** - Painting vivid pictures of dharma and consequences of inaction.

Instead of just giving logic, Krishna **wove a story** that transformed Arjuna's fear into clarity. **This is the power of storytelling in sales.**

The Storytelling Secrets Hidden in the Ramayana

A well-crafted sales story follows a structure that resonates deeply. Let's break it down using a legendary episode from the *Ramayana.*

1. The Struggle (Pain Point) - Setting the Stage

Every great story begins with a **problem**. In sales, this is the customer's **pain point**.

◈ *Example from the Ramayana:* When Lord Rama's army needed to cross the ocean to Lanka, it seemed impossible. They lacked resources, time, and a clear solution.

◈ *Sales Parallel:* A customer struggling to secure their family's future but feeling overwhelmed by financial uncertainties.

2. The Revelation (Solution) - Introducing the Hero

The turning point of any story is when a **solution emerges**.

◈ *Example from the Ramayana:* Hanuman, driven by devotion, **realized his hidden strength** and leaped across the ocean.

◈ *Sales Parallel:* Your product/service should be positioned as this revelation–**the moment the customer realizes they CAN solve their problem.**

◈ Vedic Connection:

सत्यमेव जयते नानृतं
सत्येन पन्था विततो देवयानः ।

satyam eva jayate nānṛtam
satyena panthā vitato devayānaḥ
Mundaka Upanishad 3.1.6

"Truth alone triumphs, not falsehood. The path of truth leads to the divine."

A sales story rooted in truth and authenticity will always win over customers.

How to Craft Your Own Sales Story

Want to create high-impact sales stories? Use this 4-Step Storytelling Framework:

1. Start with a relatable problem (Pain Point)

- Identify a challenge your customer faces.
- Example: "Many families struggle with saving for their child's education."

2. Introduce a hero (Real-Life Example or Scriptural Analogy)

- Use a past client, famous personality, or a character from scripture.
- Example: "Like Arjuna on the battlefield, many hesitate before making big financial decisions."

3. Present the breakthrough moment (Solution)

- Show how your product/service provides clarity and resolution.

- Example: "A customer, unsure about investing, learned how SIPs in mutual funds can secure a child's future."

4. End with transformation (Success Story)

- Showcase the impact—customer testimonials, benefits, or a vision.
- Example: "Now, he sleeps peacefully knowing his child's education is secured."

यद्यदाचरति श्रेष्ठस्तत्तदेवेतरो जनः ।
स यत्प्रमाणं कुरुते लोकस्तदनुवर्तते ॥

yad yad ācharati śhreṣṭhas tat tad evetaro janaḥ
sa yat pramāṇaṁ kurute lokas tad anuvartate

"Whatever actions great people perform, common people follow. Whatever standards they set, the world follows."

Bhagavad Gita - Chapter 3, Verse 21

As a salesperson, you set the standard. Be the storyteller that people follow, and you'll not only sell but also inspire action and transformation.

Final Takeaways & Assignment

☑ **Exercise 1:** Rewrite a failed sales pitch as a story.

☑ **Exercise 2:** Find a story from the *Mahabharata* or *Ramayana* that aligns with your product.

☑ **Exercise 3:** Record yourself narrating a sales story and analyze its impact.

Master storytelling, and you won't just sell—you'll transform lives.

Conclusion: Make Your Sales Unforgettable

Storytelling is not just a tool—it's the most **ancient, powerful, and effective** way to influence, inspire, and sell. Whether you're explaining insurance, mutual funds, or any product, stories **engage the mind and touch the heart**.

यद्यदाचरति श्रेष्ठस्तत्तदेवेतरो जनः |
स यत्प्रमाणं कुरुते लोकस्तदनुवर्तते ||

"Yad yad ācharati śhreṣṭhas tat tad evetaro janaḥ,
sa yat pramāṇaṁ kurute lokas tad anuvartate."
Bhagavad Gita - Chapter 3, Verse 21:

"Whatever actions great people perform, common people follow. Whatever standards they set, the world follows."

As a salesperson, you set the standard. Be the storyteller that people follow, and you'll not only sell but also inspire.

Chapter 8

Sealing the Deal – A Step-by-Step Guide to Winning Sales Like a Warrior

Introduction: The Final Battle in Sales

Winning a sale is like winning a war. A warrior prepares, strategizes, and executes flawlessly to achieve victory. Similarly, in sales, every conversation, objection, and negotiation is a battlefield where the right mindset, techniques, and tactics determine success.

In the ***Mahabharata*,** Arjuna stood at the battlefield of Kurukshetra, uncertain about fighting. But Krishna, through his wisdom, guided him to victory. Similarly, a salesperson must move beyond hesitation and take decisive action to seal the deal.

कर्मण्येवाधिकारस्ते मा फलेषु कदाचन |
मा कर्मफलहेतुर्भूर्मा ते सङ्गोऽस्त्वकर्मणि ||

"Karmanye vadhikaraste ma phaleshu kadachana,
ma karma phala hetur bhur ma te sangostva akarmani."
Bhagavad Gita – Chapter 2, Verse 47:

"You have a right to perform your duty, but never to the fruits of your work. Let not the fruits of action be your motive, nor let your attachment be to inaction."

This verse teaches us a key lesson in sales: Focus on the process, not just the outcome. When you follow a structured approach, success follows naturally.

The Stages of a Sales Cycle: The Warrior's Path to Victory

A great warrior never goes into battle without a plan. Similarly, a salesperson must master every step of the sales cycle to ensure a smooth close.

1. Prospecting: Identifying the Right Battlefield

In the *Ramayana*, when Lord Rama needed to cross the ocean to reach Lanka, he didn't rush into battle blindly. He first assessed the situation, sought advice, and strategized.

Similarly, in sales, prospecting is about choosing the right battlefield–identifying potential customers who genuinely need your solution.

Rig Veda 1.89.1:

आ नो भद्राः क्रतवो यन्तु विश्वतोऽदब्धासो

"Aano bhadra krtavo yantu vishwatah."
"Let noble thoughts come to us from all directions."

◈ Actionable Tip: Use social media, referrals, and networking to find the right customers. Don't waste time chasing unqualified leads.

2. Building Rapport: Gaining Trust Before the Battle

Before Krishna guided Arjuna, he built a deep bond of trust with him. This made Arjuna receptive to Krishna's wisdom.

In sales, before pitching, you must build trust with the prospect. If they trust you, they will buy from you.

◈ Actionable Tip:

- Show genuine interest in the customer's needs.
- Listen more than you speak.
- Use personal stories to build emotional connections.

यद्यदाचरति श्रेष्ठस्तत्तदेवेतरो जनः ।
स यत्प्रमाणं कुरुते लोकस्तदनुवर्तते ।।

"Yad yad ācharati śhreṣhthas tat tad evetaro janaḥ,
sa yat pramāṇaṁ kurute lokas tad anuvartate."
Bhagavad Gita – Chapter 3, Verse 21:

"Whatever actions great people perform, common people follow. Whatever standards they set, the world follows."

A salesperson must lead the conversation with authenticity so the prospect follows.

3. Understanding Customer Buying Triggers: The 'Why' Behind the 'Yes'

A sale happens when you hit the right emotional and logical triggers.

The Mahabharata gives us a great example of this: When Karna was hesitant to give up his divine armor, Indra (in disguise) triggered his generosity by praising his reputation as a giver. Karna, unable to resist, gave it away.

Similarly, a salesperson must understand the real trigger behind a customer's decision.

◈ Common Buying Triggers:

✔ Fear of missing out (FOMO)

✔ Desire for security (especially in insurance and investments)

✔ Need for recognition (luxury and premium products)

✔ Urgency (limited-time offers)

Yajur Veda 40.1:

ईशा वास्यमिदं सर्वं यत्किञ्च जगत्यां जगत्।

"Isha vasyam idam sarvam yat kincha jagatyam jagat."
"Everything in this universe is connected and interdependent."

A buyer's decision is not just about the product; it's about their deeper needs. Learn to uncover these triggers.

Handling Objections with Confidence: The Arjuna Mindset

Every customer will have objections. Just like Arjuna hesitated to fight, customers hesitated to buy. A great salesperson, like Krishna, must remove their doubts with wisdom.

Common Objections & How to Handle Them

☑ "It's too expensive."

◈ Response: Instead of justifying the price, show the long-term value.

📃 *Example:* "Think of it like planting a seed. You invest now, and it grows into a tree that gives shade and fruit for years to come."

☑ "I need time to think."

◈ Response: Create urgency without being pushy.

📃 *Example:* "Imagine if Lord Rama had delayed his decision to go to Lanka. Delay often leads to missed opportunities. Let's ensure you don't miss out on the benefits of this today."

☑ "I need to discuss with my spouse."

◈ Response: Involve the spouse in the discussion.

📃 *Example:* "Even in the Mahabharata, great warriors like Bhishma took counsel before making decisions. Would you like me to explain this to both of you so you can make the best choice together?"

इति ते ज्ञानमाख्यातं गुह्याद्गुह्यतरं मया |
विमृश्यैतदशेषेण यथेच्छसि तथा कुरु ||

"Iti te jñānam ākhyātaṁ guhyād guhyataraṁ mayā,
vimṛśyaitad aśeṣeṇa yathecchasi tathā kuru."
Bhagavad Gita – Chapter 18, Verse 63:

"I have explained to you the most confidential knowledge. Now reflect deeply and do as you wish."

Handling objections is not about forcing a decision; it's about helping the prospect gain clarity.

Closing Techniques Inspired by Ancient Scriptures

Closing is the moment of truth. It's when you either win the deal or lose it.

1. The 'Bhishma' Close: The Power of Commitment

Bhishma took the vow of celibacy and never broke it. Similarly, if you can get your prospect to verbally commit, the deal is almost closed.

📃 *Example:* "On a scale of 1 to 10, how sure are you about this? If it's an 8 or higher, let's move forward."

2. The 'Krishna' Close: The Art of Persuasion

Krishna convince Arjuna to fight by painting a vivid picture of duty, legacy, and impact.

📃 *Example:* "Think about the peace of mind your family will have with this insurance. This is not just a policy–it's a promise of security."

मयि सर्वाणि कर्माणि संन्यस्याध्यात्मचेतसा |
निराशीर्निर्ममो भूत्वा युध्यस्व विगतज्वरः ||

"Mayi sarvāṇi karmāṇi sannyasyādhyātma-chetasā,
nirāśīr nirmamo bhūtvā yudhyasva vigata-jvaraḥ."
Bhagavad Gita - Chapter 3, Verse 30:

"Dedicate all your actions to me with full knowledge of the self, without desire or selfishness, and fight without hesitation."

In sales, fight without hesitation. Believe in your product, and your customer will too.

Actionable Steps & Assignment

✅ Exercise 1: Identify three objections you commonly face. Write down a powerful response using a story from scriptures.

☑ Exercise 2: Practice the 'Bhishma Close' and 'Krishna Close' with a colleague.

☑ Exercise 3: Record your closing pitch and analyze your confidence level.

Conclusion: The Sales Warrior's Code

Sales is not just about closing deals. It's about serving customers, solving problems, and building trust–just like great warriors served a greater cause.

उद्धरेदात्मनात्मानं नात्मानमवसादयेत् |

"Uddhared ātmanātmānaṁ na ātmānam avasādayet."
Bhagavad Gita – Chapter 6, Verse 5:

"Elevate yourself through your own efforts. Do not degrade yourself."

A true sales warrior never gives up. Go forth, win deals, and change lives.

Chapter 9

Mastering Objection Handling: Turning 'No' into 'Yes'

Introduction: The Art of Handling Resistance

Every salesperson, no matter how skilled, faces objections. A 'no' is never a final rejection–it's an opportunity to uncover hidden doubts, reframe perspectives, and ultimately **turn resistance into acceptance**.

In the Bhagavad Gita, when Arjuna hesitated on the battlefield, Krishna didn't dismiss his concerns outright. Instead, he guided him by addressing his doubts with wisdom, logic, and conviction:

उद्धरेदात्मनात्मानं नात्मानमवसादयेत् |
आत्मैव ह्यात्मनो बन्धुरात्मैव रिपुरात्मन: ||

"Uddhared ātmanātmānaṁ na ātmānam avasādayet।
Ātmaiva hyātmano bandhurātmaiva ripurātmanaḥ॥"
(Bhagavad Gita 6.5)

"One must elevate oneself by one's own mind and not degrade oneself. The mind is a friend to one who masters it, and an enemy to one who fails to control it."

Objections in sales, like Arjuna's doubts, arise from **fear, misunderstanding, or incomplete knowledge**. As sales professionals, our role is to **help prospects elevate their thinking**, address their fears, and guide them to an informed decision.

Understanding the Root of Objections

Objections usually fall into five categories:

1. **Lack of Need** - "I don't need this product."
2. **Lack of Trust** - "I don't believe in your company."
3. **Lack of Urgency** - "I'll think about it later."
4. **Lack of Money** - "It's too expensive."
5. **Lack of Information** - "I need more details."

Each of these objections can be **decoded and resolved**, just as Krishna decoded Arjuna's hesitation and turned his uncertainty into **absolute conviction.**

Story from the Ramayana: Hanuman and the Hidden Strength

When Lakshmana was severely wounded in battle, the only cure was the **Sanjeevani herb** from the Himalayas. But when Hanuman was sent to retrieve it, he faced **doubt, resistance, and obstacles** at every step.

1. **Doubt** (Lack of Information): He wasn't sure where the herb was.

2. **Objection from Guards** (Lack of Trust): The enemy's forces tried to stop him.
3. **Time Sensitivity (Urgency Objection)**: Lakshmana's life was at stake.

Hanuman's response? **He didn't argue—he acted.** Instead of wasting time searching, he lifted the entire mountain!

Lesson for Salespeople:

If a customer hesitates, don't fight the resistance—**change the approach.** Instead of arguing about price, demonstrate **value** so convincingly that they see no other choice.

Techniques for Handling Objections

1. The Bhagavad Gita Approach: Educate, Don't Argue

When Arjuna hesitated, Krishna didn't force him—he enlightened him. Salespeople must do the same.

✅ **Instead of:** "This product is better than others."

✅ **Try:** "Let me share why thousands of customers trust this product..."

This method uses **social proof and education** rather than aggressive selling.

2. The Mirror Technique: Empathize First

When a customer says, "It's too expensive," instead of arguing, respond with:

✅ "I completely understand. Many of our happiest customers felt the same way at first. But here's what they discovered..."

This technique mirrors their concern, making them more open to listening.

3. The 'Feel-Felt-Found' Strategy

This classic technique helps prospects see a new perspective.

✔ **Feel** - Acknowledge their concern: "I understand how you feel."

✔ **Felt** - Relate to others who felt the same way: "Many customers felt the same."

✔ **Found** - Present a solution: "Here's what they found after using our product..."

4. The Vedic Way: Answer with a Question

The **Upanishads and Vedas** teach through **questions and counter-questions**. Instead of arguing, **ask a powerful question** that shifts the prospect's thinking.

☑ **Customer:** "I don't think I need this."

☑ **Salesperson:** "I understand. But if you could improve one thing in your current setup, what would it be?"

This technique **makes the customer think differently** instead of simply rejecting your offer.

Real-Life Case Study: Turning a Skeptic into a Client

A life insurance advisor once faced a wealthy client who said, **"I don't need life insurance. I have investments."**

Instead of pushing back, the advisor used the **Bhagavad Gita Approach:**

✅ **Step 1 (Educate):** "Many of our high-net-worth clients thought the same. But they realized that while investments build wealth, insurance **protects it**."

✅ **Step 2 (Mirror & Feel-Felt-Found):** "One of my clients felt the same, but when a sudden crisis hit, he saw how insurance saved his family's future."

✅ **Step 3 (Vedic Questioning):** "If a financial crisis hit tomorrow, which of your assets could your family use immediately?"

By the end of the conversation, the client saw **insurance not as an expense, but as protection**—and he purchased a policy.

Actionable Takeaways & Assignments

📌 **Assignment 1: Reframe an Objection:** Pick a common sales objection you hear often (e.g., "It's too expensive") and write **three different ways** to handle it using:

- The Bhagavad Gita approach (Education)
- The Feel-Felt-Found technique
- The Vedic Questioning method

📌 **Assignment 2: Role-Play Challenge:** Pair up with a colleague. One plays the customer, the other the salesperson. The goal: **Handle 5 different objections in 5 minutes** using different techniques.

📌 **Assignment 3: The Hanuman Test:** Think of a tough sales challenge you are facing. How can you change your approach rather than fight resistance? Write your new strategy.

Final Thoughts: Turning 'No' into 'Yes' is a Skill You Can Master

Objections are not rejections; they are **hidden requests for more information.** By using:

✅ **Bhagavad Gita wisdom** (Educate, don't argue)

✅ **Ramayana insights** (Change the approach like Hanuman)

✅ **Proven sales techniques** (Feel-Felt-Found, Vedic Questions)

You can **transform hesitation into agreement and doubt into conviction**–just like Krishna transformed Arjuna's uncertainty into unwavering determination.

तस्मादज्ञानसम्भूतं हृत्स्थं ज्ञानासिनात्मनः |
छित्त्वैनं संशयं योगमातिष्ठोत्तिष्ठ भारत ||

"Tasmād ajñānasambhūtaṁ hṛtsthaṁ jñānāsinātmanaḥ।
Chittvainam saṁśayaṁ yogam ātiṣṭhottistha bhārata॥"
(Bhagavad Gita 4.42)

"Therefore, with the sword of knowledge, cut off this doubt in your heart. Arise, O Arjuna, and engage in action."

Just as Arjuna rose with clarity and purpose, every salesperson can **turn objections into opportunities** and achieve success.

Chapter 10

Building Long-Term Client Relationships for Repeat Sales and Referrals

Introduction: The Power of Relationship Selling

A single sale may bring revenue, but a strong relationship brings repeat business, referrals, and lifelong loyalty. The best salespeople do not just close deals; they build trust and create lasting bonds—just as great leaders, warriors, and kings did in our ancient scriptures.

The *Ramayana* and *Mahabharata* teach us that trust and loyalty are the foundation of lasting relationships. Lord Rama's bond with Hanuman, Krishna's unwavering support for Arjuna, and the loyalty between Karna and Duryodhana all reveal key lessons in relationship management.

ऋग्वेदः १.७.९

"संगच्छध्वं संवदध्वं सं वो मनांसि जानताम्।"

saṃgacchadhvaṃ saṃvadadhvaṃ saṃ vo manāṃsi jānatām

"Move together, speak in one voice, and let your minds be united in understanding."

This Vedic wisdom teaches us that successful relationships, whether in life or business, are built on alignment, mutual respect, and shared purpose.

Why Client Relationships Matter More Than Ever

In today's fast-paced world, customers have numerous options. Why should they stay loyal to you? Because people don't just buy products—they buy trust, experience, and connection.

Benefits of Strong Client Relationships:

✔ Repeat Sales - Loyal customers come back.

✔ Referrals - Happy clients bring new clients.

✔ Higher Lifetime Value - A returning client is more profitable than acquiring a new one.

✔ Brand Advocacy - Your clients become your promoters.

महाभारतम् ५.१२०.१३

"विश्वासात् मित्रमाप्नोति विश्वासात् सुखमश्नुते।"

Vishwasat Mitramapnoti Vishwasat Sukhamashnute

"Through trust, one gains friendship; through trust, one attains happiness."

◈ Actionable Tip: Start seeing your customers as partners, not transactions. The stronger the trust, the deeper the loyalty.

How to Turn First-Time Buyers into Lifelong Clients

Many salespeople make the mistake of focusing only on closing deals. But the real work begins after the sale.

1. Deliver More Than Promised

In the *Ramayana*, when Lord Rama accepted Vibhishana (Ravana's brother) as an ally, he didn't just promise protection–he treated him like family.

📜 *Sales Lesson:* Never just meet expectations–exceed them. Surprise your clients with extra value.

◈ Actionable Tip: Offer free insights, resources, or small gestures of appreciation. A simple thank-you note or unexpected bonus builds goodwill.

2. The Art of Staying in Touch Without Being Pushy

Staying in touch is crucial, but how do you do it without seeming like you're just trying to sell? The secret lies in genuine connection.

In the *Mahabharata*, Krishna stayed connected with the Pandavas not just during war, but in their times of joy and sorrow. Similarly, a salesperson must engage beyond business.

श्रीमद्भगवद्गीता १७.१५

अनुद्वेगकरं वाक्यं सत्यं प्रियहितं च यत् |

anudvega-karaṁ vākyaṁ satyaṁ priya-hitaṁ cha yat

"Speak words that are true, pleasant, and beneficial."

📃 *Sales Lesson:* Stay in touch with relevant, valuable communication rather than just sales pitches.

◈ Ways to Stay Connected:

✔ Send a festive greeting or birthday wish.

✔ Share useful content (industry insights, articles, tips).

✔ Congratulate them on their achievements.

✔ Offer personalized recommendations based on past purchases.

The Ramayana's Lessons on Loyalty and Trust

The *Ramayana* is full of powerful lessons on relationship-building. Let's look at three examples that can be applied to client management.

1. Lord Rama & Hanuman – The Power of Genuine Appreciation

When Hanuman returned from Lanka with news of Sita, Lord Rama was so overwhelmed with gratitude that he embraced Hanuman as an equal.

रामायणम् ६.१.१९

"कृतज्ञो मित्रभक्तश्च यस्याहं प्रियताम् गतः।"

"A person who is grateful and devoted to friends wins love and loyalty in return."

📃 *Sales Lesson:* Express gratitude and recognition. Acknowledge your clients' loyalty.

◈ Actionable Tip: Send a handwritten thank-you note or a small token of appreciation to your best customers.

2. Vibhishana's Trust in Rama – Rewarding Those Who Believe in You

Vibhishana, Ravana's brother, left Lanka to seek refuge with Lord Rama. Even when Rama's allies doubted Vibhishana's loyalty, Rama welcomed him without hesitation.

📜 *Sales Lesson:* Reward loyal clients who trust you—whether it's through exclusive benefits, VIP treatment, or early access to new offers.

◈ Actionable Tip: Identify your most loyal clients and offer them priority service or special perks.

3. Bharat's Devotion – Unwavering Commitment

Even when Lord Rama was exiled, Bharat ruled Ayodhya not as a king, but as a caretaker, ensuring the kingdom remained loyal to Rama.

📜 *Sales Lesson:* Stand by your clients even when they're not buying.

◈ Actionable Tip: If a client hasn't purchased in a while, check in—not to sell, but to show you care.

The Referral Effect: How Strong Relationships Bring New Clients

Referrals are the highest quality leads, and they come naturally when customers trust you. But most salespeople don't ask for referrals the right way.

यजुर्वेदः २०.२९

"ददाति प्रतिगृह्णाति मैत्री चोपजायते।"

Dadati pratigrahnati maitri chop javate

"Giving and receiving create bonds of friendship."

📜 *Sales Lesson:* If you've provided value, don't hesitate to ask for referrals—but do it at the right time and in the right way.

◈ How to Ask for Referrals Naturally:

✔ Ask after delivering great service, not before.

✔ Say, "Who else do you know that I can help in the same way?"

✔ Offer an incentive, like a discount or free service, to both the referrer and the new customer.

Actionable Steps & Assignment

☑ Exercise 1: List your top 5 clients. Identify one way to delight them unexpectedly this week.

☑ Exercise 2: Write down three personalized ways you can stay in touch with a client without selling.

☑ Exercise 3: Identify one happy client and ask them for a referral today.

Conclusion: Sales is Not About Transactions—It's About Trust

Building long-term client relationships is not about making a sale today—it's about creating trust that lasts a lifetime.

श्रीमद्भगवद्गीता १२.१४

सन्तुष्ट: सततं योगी यतात्मा दृढनिश्चय: |

santuṣhṭaḥ satataṁ yogī yatātmā dṛiḍha-niśhchayaḥ

"The one who is ever content, self-controlled, and firm in resolve attains success."

If you prioritize relationships over revenue, the revenue will take care of itself. Serve first, sell second.

Now go forth and build relationships that last a lifetime!

Chapter 11

The Science of Negotiation – Winning Without Losing

Introduction: The Art of Negotiation in Sales

Negotiation is at the heart of every successful sale. Whether you're closing a deal, handling objections, or discussing pricing, your ability to **negotiate effectively** determines your success. But negotiation isn't just about winning–it's about **creating value for both sides.**

Bhagavad Gita teaches us:

"Vigyanam sa vijnanam yat jñatvā mokṣyase'śubhāt" (Bhagavad Gita 9.1)

"This knowledge, combined with wisdom, shall liberate you from all misfortune."

Just like Arjuna needed **both knowledge and wisdom** to win battles, sales professionals need **both strategy and psychology** to negotiate effectively.

The Power of Strategic Negotiation: A Lesson from Mahabharata

One of the greatest negotiators in history was **Krishna**. Before the Kurukshetra war, he went to the Kaurava court as a peace envoy, hoping to negotiate and avoid war. He used every tactic:

✔ **Persuasion** - Appealing to Duryodhana's wisdom

✔ **Logic & Facts** - Showing the consequences of war

✔ **Emotion** - Reminding them of dharma

But Duryodhana refused to budge. Krishna then understood: Some negotiations are destined to fail, and walking away is the best choice.

Key Negotiation Principles from Krishna

1. **Know Your BATNA (Best Alternative to a Negotiated Agreement)**
    - Krishna knew that if peace talks failed, war was inevitable—so he prepared both paths.
    - In sales, always have a backup plan—if the client refuses, what's your next move?
2. **Control the Frame**
    - Krishna entered the court as a negotiator but left as a divine figure, influencing the audience.
    - In sales, control how the client sees your offer—position it as a solution, not just a product.
3. **Silence is a Negotiation Weapon**
    - Krishna often used silence to make others reveal their true intentions.

- In sales, silence after a pricing objection makes the client reconsider before rejecting.

Modern Sales Negotiation: Real-Life Case Studies

Case Study 1: The Power of Reciprocity

A car dealership once offered free service for a year to potential buyers. This **act of goodwill** made customers feel obligated to reciprocate by purchasing the car.

✔ Bhagavad Gita Insight:

यज्ञार्थात्कर्मणोऽन्यत्र लोकोऽयं कर्मबन्धनः |

"Yajñārthāt karmaṇo'nyatra loko'yaṁ karma-bandhanaḥ"

(BG 3.9)
"Selfless action frees one from bondage."

Lesson:
Offer something valuable first—advice, free consultation, or additional service—to make customers more inclined to say **yes**.

Case Study 2: The Anchor Effect in Pricing

A furniture company displayed an expensive ₹1,00,000 sofa **next to** a ₹50,000 one. Customers saw the second as a **great deal**, leading to **higher sales**.

✔ **Chanakya Niti:**

"First set the expectation high, then make your actual offer seem like a bargain."

Lesson:
Always start with a **higher offer**, then negotiate down to make the client feel they are getting a great deal.

The Science of Persuasion: Psychological Techniques in Negotiation

1. Anchoring Effect

✔ People rely too much on the **first number** presented.
✔ If you start high, the client's counteroffer will also be **higher**.

☑ **Example:** Instead of saying, *"Our service costs ₹20,000,"* say, "Most clients pay ₹30,000 for this, but I can offer it for ₹20,000."_

2. Mirroring

✔ People trust those who **subtly mimic their tone & body language**.

✔ When clients lean forward, **you lean forward**; when they cross arms, **you do the same**.

☑ Example: A study showed mirroring increased closing rates by 17% in negotiations.

3. The Power of Silence

✔ When a client says, "That's too expensive," don't rush to justify.

✔ Stay silent and **let them fill the gap**–they might talk themselves into the deal!

☑ **Example:** A real estate agent who used silence saw **a 22% increase in deal closures.**

Negotiation Lessons from the Ramayana

Lesson 1: Hanuman's Diplomacy with Ravana

When Hanuman entered Ravana's court as Rama's messenger, he:

✔ **Spoke calmly** but firmly.

✔ **Used logic** before emotion.

✔ **Kept Rama's power in reserve (BATNA).**

✔ **Bhagavad Gita Insight:**

"Anāsaktaḥ buddhiḥ yasyāstīha sa muktaḥ" (BG 5.3)
"One who stays detached but strategic is truly liberated."

☑ Sales Application: Never show desperation. Always negotiate from a position of strength.

Actionable Steps & Assignments

1. The Krishna Negotiation Exercise

💡 **Scenario:** A client says, *"Your price is too high."*

👉 Write down **three different responses**:

- One using **logic** (facts & figures)
- One using **emotion** (storytelling & impact)
- One using **reciprocity** (offering something in return)

2. The Silent Close Challenge

🚀 **Goal:** Next time a client objects, **stay silent for 5 seconds.**

💡 **Observe:** Does the client **justify their objection**, or do they rethink their stance?

Conclusion: Becoming a Negotiation Master

Negotiation is not about winning or losing–it's about creating long-term value. By learning from Krishna, Chanakya, Hanuman, and modern psychology, you can persuade, influence, and close deals effectively.

✔ Final Bhagavad Gita Wisdom:

समत्वं योग उच्यते |

"Samatvam yoga ucyate" (BG 2.48)

"True wisdom is maintaining balance in all situations."

☑ **Takeaway:** Approach every negotiation **calmly, strategically, and ethically**, and success will follow.

Chapter 12

The Dharma of Sales – Ethics, Integrity, and Long-Term Success

"When wealth is lost, nothing is lost. When health is lost, something is lost. But when character is lost, everything is lost."

– Chanakya

Why Ethical Selling Leads to Lasting Success

Many salespeople focus only on short-term gains–closing a deal, hitting targets, and making quick commissions. But true sales mastery lies in long-term success, where trust and integrity build **a lasting reputation, repeat business, and referrals**.

A Rainmaker knows that deception, pressure tactics, or manipulation may bring **temporary victories**, but in the long run, they erode trust and damage credibility.

In the **Mahabharata**, the contrast between **Yudhishthira and Duryodhana** shows the power of ethics in leadership and business. While Duryodhana used **deception and unfair means** to acquire wealth and power, Yudhishthira's commitment to Dharma **earned him respect, trust, and a lasting legacy**.

Krishna explains the importance of ethical action in the Bhagavad Gita:

"न हि कश्चित्क्षणमपि जातु तिष्ठत्यकर्मकृत्।
कार्यते ह्यवशः कर्म सर्वः प्रकृतिजैर्गुणैः॥"

na hi kaśhchit kṣhaṇam api jātu tiṣhṭhatyakarma-kṛit
kāryate hyavaśhaḥ karma sarvaḥ prakṛiti-jair guṇaiḥ
(Bhagavad Gita 3.5)

"No one can remain inactive even for a moment. Everyone is compelled to act according to their nature."

This means that actions define us—and ethical actions build a solid foundation for long-term success.

Lessons from Yudhishthira: Honesty in Business

Yudhishthira, the eldest of the Pandavas, was known as *Dharma Raj*—the king of righteousness. He refused to compromise his integrity, even in difficult situations.

The Dice Game: A Test of Ethical Strength

During the infamous **game of dice**, Yudhishthira made a grave mistake by gambling away everything—including his kingdom, his brothers, and even Draupadi. But even when he realized he was **tricked by Shakuni's deception**, he **accepted his loss with honor**, showing his deep commitment to **truth and fairness**.

In contrast, Duryodhana and Shakuni **won through manipulation**, but their unethical approach led to **destruction and war**.

Lesson for Salespeople:

- **Never sell through deception** – Misleading clients may win deals today, but it destroys your reputation tomorrow.
- **Be honest about your product's strengths and limitations** – Customers respect transparency and will trust you more.
- **Your word is your bond** – Always deliver what you promise, and your clients will remain loyal.

Krishna reinforces this principle:

"सत्यमेव जयते नानृतं सत्येन पन्था विततो देवयानः।"

satyameva jayate nānṛtaṁ satyena panthā vitato devayānaḥ
(Mundaka Upanishad 3.1.6)

"Truth alone triumphs, not falsehood. The path of truth leads to success and divine progress."

How Trust and Credibility Build Unstoppable Momentum

A trustworthy salesperson doesn't just close deals; they build long-term relationships.

Case Study: The Wealthy Merchant and His Honest Assistant

In ancient India, a wealthy merchant hired an assistant to help with business. One day, while traveling, they found **a bag of gold coins** on the roadside.

The assistant suggested they take it, but the merchant refused, saying:
"If the owner comes searching, he will trust us more if we return it. Wealth earned dishonestly never stays."

A week later, the rightful owner of the gold returned. Overwhelmed by the merchant's honesty, he gave him double the amount in gratitude and made him his exclusive supplier.

Lesson for Salespeople:

- **Trust takes time to build but seconds to lose** - Always choose integrity over short-term gain.
- **A good reputation brings more business** - Happy clients refer you to others.
- **Ethical salespeople attract high-value clients** - Businesses prefer to work with people they trust.

Krishna confirms this principle:

"यद्यदाचरति श्रेष्ठस्तत्तदेवेतरो जनः।
स यत्प्रमाणं कुरुते लोकस्तदनुवर्तते॥"

yad yad ācharati śhreṣhṭhas tat tad evetaro janaḥ
sa yat pramāṇaṁ kurute lokas tad anuvartate
(Bhagavad Gita 3.21)

"People follow the standards set by great individuals. Whatever they do, others will follow."

The Ramayana's Lesson: Why Ravana Lost Everything

Ravana, the mighty king of Lanka, had **power, intelligence, and unmatched resources**. Yet he lost everything because he chose greed over righteousness.

When he kidnapped Sita, he ignored multiple warnings from:

- His brother **Vibhishana** (who later defected to Rama's side),

- His wife **Mandodari,**
- Even **Lord Brahma himself.**

His unethical choices led to his downfall, proving that:

"धर्म एव हतो हन्ति धर्मो रक्षति रक्षितः।"

dharma eva hato hanti dharmo rakṣhati rakṣhitaḥ
(Manusmriti 8.15)

"One who destroys Dharma is destroyed by Dharma itself. One who upholds Dharma is protected by it."

Sales Takeaways from Ravana's Mistake:

- **Greedy sales tactics backfire** – Pushing unnecessary products damages long-term relationships.
- **Listen to ethical advisors** – If mentors or colleagues warn against a tactic, reconsider your approach.
- **Customers remember who deceived them** – Short-term wins through dishonesty lead to future losses.

How to Apply Dharma in Sales: Practical Guidelines

A **Rainmaker** follows Dharma in sales by:

1. **Selling with Authenticity**
   - Understand your client's real needs before offering a solution.
   - Recommend the **right product**, even if it means a smaller sale.
2. **Building Relationships, Not Just Transactions**
   - Follow up **after** the sale to ensure satisfaction.

- Help clients even when you're not selling something.

3. **Standing by Your Commitments**
   - If you promise a benefit, a feature, or a delivery timeline, ensure you fulfill it.
   - Honesty leads to referrals, repeat business, and credibility.

4. **Avoiding Pressure Tactics**
   - A desperate salesperson pressures customers. A Rainmaker **guides and educates** them.
   - If a client says no, **respect their decision and keep the door open for the future**.

Final Thought: Dharma Always Wins

In sales, Dharma always wins in the end. An ethical salesperson may not close deals as fast as a manipulative one, but over time, their reputation grows, their network expands, and their business flourishes.

Krishna gives the ultimate assurance:

"मन्मना भव मद्भक्तो मद्याजी मां नमस्कुरु।
मामेवैष्यसि सत्यं ते प्रतिजाने प्रियोऽसि मे॥"

(Bhagavad Gita 18.65)

"If you act with faith, sincerity, and devotion, success will follow."

The world remembers **Yudhishthira, not Duryodhana**.

The world respects **Rama, not Ravana**.

And in sales, customers return to **trusted advisors, not manipulators**.

Be a **Rainmaker with Dharma**, and success will follow you effortlessly.

Chapter 13

Understanding Customer Karma – How to Match the Right Product to the Right Person

"Not every customer is your customer. The right product at the right time, to the right person, leads to true sales success."

Introduction: The Law of Alignment in Sales

In the Bhagavad Gita, Krishna emphasizes the importance of Svadharma–one's natural duty or purpose. He says:

"श्रेयान्स्वधर्मो विगुणः परधर्मात्स्वनुष्ठितात्।
स्वधर्मे निधनं श्रेयः परधर्मो भयावहः॥"

"śhreyān swa-dharmo viguṇaḥ para-dharmāt sv-anuṣhṭhitāt,
swa-dharme nidhanaṁ śhreyaḥ para-dharmo bhayāvahaḥ"
(Bhagavad Gita 3.35)

"It is better to follow one's own path imperfectly than to follow another's path perfectly. It is better to die performing one's own duty than to follow another's path, which is fraught with fear."

This verse teaches that alignment is the key to success. In sales, this means matching the right product to the right person instead of trying to sell something to everyone. Just as every individual has a unique Dharma (duty), every customer has a unique need.

A Rainmaker does not force a sale; they align the product with the customer's true requirements. This is the essence of Customer Karma–offering solutions that truly serve the prospect.

---

1. Not Every Customer is Your Customer

One of the biggest mistakes salespeople make is trying to sell to everyone. But in reality, not every person is a good fit for your product or service.

Case Study: The Archer's Target

In the Mahabharata, Dronacharya once asked his students to shoot a bird on a tree. Before allowing them to release their arrows, he asked what they could see.

- One student said, "I see the sky, the tree, and the bird."
- Another said, "I see the branch, the leaves, and the bird."
- But when Arjuna was asked, he said, "I see only the bird's eye."

Dronacharya smiled and allowed him to shoot, and Arjuna hit the target perfectly.

This lesson is critical in sales—targeting the right customer is key. If you try to sell to everyone, you will fail. A Rainmaker identifies their ideal customer and focuses only on them.

How to Identify the Right Customer?

1. **Need Alignment** – Does the customer have a genuine need for your product?
2. **Ability to Buy** – Can they afford it? Are they decision-makers?
3. **Timing** – Is this the right time for them to buy?

Krishna explains:

"सर्वधर्मान्परित्यज्य मामेकं शरणं व्रज। "

"Give up all doubts and surrender to the truth." (Bhagavad Gita 18.66)

In sales, instead of wasting energy on the wrong prospects, surrender to the truth—focus only on qualified leads.

---

2. The Dharma of Selling: Offering What is Right, Not What is Easy

A dishonest salesperson sells anything to anyone. A Rainmaker sells only what truly benefits the customer.

Example: Yudhishthira and the Power of Truth

During the Mahabharata war, Yudhishthira was known for his truthfulness. Even when Krishna suggested he bend the truth strategically, Yudhishthira hesitated. He understood that truth must not be manipulated for short-term gain.

Similarly, in sales, short-term tricks may work, but long-term success comes from honesty and alignment. If you push a wrong product, the customer may buy once, but they will never return.

How to Ensure Ethical Selling?

- **Educate, don't manipulate** – Teach customers about their best options.
- **Sell benefits, not just features** – How does the product solve their specific problem?
- **Reject misaligned deals** – If a customer is not the right fit, walk away.

Krishna says:

"न मे पार्थास्ति कर्तव्यं त्रिषु लोकेषु किंचन। "

"I have nothing to gain, yet I act for the welfare of all."
(Bhagavad Gita 3.22)

A true salesperson acts not for personal gain but for customer benefit.

---

3. Karma and Sales: Understanding the Customer's Readiness

Not every customer is ready to buy, even if they are a good fit.

The Ripening of Fruit – A Lesson from Nature

In the Bhagavad Gita, Krishna describes how everything happens at the right time:

"कालोऽस्मि लोकक्षयकृत्प्रवृद्धो"

"I am Time, the great destroyer of the worlds."
(Bhagavad Gita 11.32)

A mango cannot be eaten when it is green. It must ripen. Similarly, a customer must be in the right stage of their buying journey.

How to Identify Customer Readiness?

- **Early Stage (Curious)** – They are gathering information. Educate them.
- **Middle Stage (Interested)** – They are considering options. Guide them.
- **Late Stage (Ready)** – They are prepared to buy. Close the deal.

Just as Krishna waited for Arjuna to be ready before revealing the Gita, a Rainmaker waits for the customer to be ready before closing the sale.

---

4. Selling with Compassion: The Hanuman Approach

Hanuman is a perfect example of compassionate selling.

When he found Sita in Lanka, he didn't force her to leave.

Instead, he:

1. Understood her pain (listened).
2. Gave reassurance (built trust).
3. Showed proof (gave Rama's ring).

A Rainmaker sells the same way:

1. Listen deeply – Understand the customer's concerns.
2. Build trust – Show that you genuinely care.
3. Provide proof – Demonstrate how the product works for them.

Krishna teaches:

"अद्वेष्टा सर्वभूतानां मैत्रः करुण एव च।"

"Be free from envy, be friendly, and be compassionate to all" (Bhagavad Gita 12.13)

Great salespeople serve first, sell second.

---

5. The Ultimate Sales Filter: Matching the Right Customer to the Right Product

A Rainmaker does not chase customers—they attract them by offering the right solutions.

The 3-Step Customer Karma Strategy

1. Qualify before you pitch – Don't waste time on mismatched leads.
2. Align product to customer needs – Sell only what they truly require.
3. Follow up with value – Keep nurturing the relationship.

Case Study: The Village Story

A wise teacher once had two students selling lamps.

- The first student forced people to buy and made many sales.
- The second only sold to those who needed light.

Years later, the first student had no customers left. The second had a thriving business—because he sold with alignment.

Krishna says:

"तस्मादसक्तः सततं कार्यं कर्म समाचर।"

"Therefore, act without attachment, focusing only on your duty." (Bhagavad Gita 3.19)

A Rainmaker sells not for commission but for contribution.

Conclusion: Sales as a Sacred Duty

Matching the right product to the right person is not just a strategy—it is a duty.

Krishna's final words to Arjuna:

"कर्मण्येवाधिकारस्ते मा फलेषु कदाचन।"

"You have the right to work, but never to the fruits of work." (Bhagavad Gita 2.47)

A Rainmaker follows this wisdom—focus on the right customers, provide the right value, and trust that success will follow.

This is the true path of Customer Karma.

Chapter 14

The Energy of Money – How to Attract Wealth in Sales

"Money is never just money. It is energy, a flow of value, an exchange of effort and service. The more you understand its spiritual dimension, the more you attract it effortlessly."

Understanding Wealth from an Ancient Perspective

In modern times, money is often seen as a mere transaction, a means to acquire goods and services. However, ancient Indian wisdom viewed wealth not just as physical currency but as a form of energy–Lakshmi. The goddess of wealth, Lakshmi, represents prosperity, abundance, and fortune, but she does not stay where there is greed, dishonesty, or stagnation. Instead, she flows toward those who create, serve, and contribute.

In the Bhagavad Gita, Krishna explains:

"यज्ञार्थात्कर्मणोऽन्यत्र लोकोऽयं कर्मबन्धनः।
तदर्थं कर्म कौन्तेय मुक्तसङ्गः समाचर॥"
(Bhagavad Gita 3.9)

"All actions, when performed as a sacrifice (for the greater good), free one from the bondage of karma. Work done for selfish reasons, however, binds a person to the material world."

Sales is no different. When you approach money with fear or desperation, it moves away from you. But when you see sales as an exchange of value, helping others while staying true to ethical principles, money flows effortlessly.

Shifting from Scarcity to Abundance

Many salespeople struggle with pricing fears, negotiation anxiety, or feeling unworthy of high earnings. This stems from a scarcity mindset–thinking that wealth is limited or that charging high prices is unfair.

However, Vedic texts teach us that abundance is the natural state of the universe.

The Isha Upanishad declares:

"ईशा वास्यमिदं सर्वं यत्किञ्च जगत्यां जगत्।
तेन त्यक्तेन भुञ्जीथा मा गृधः कस्यस्विद्धनम्॥"

"The entire universe is pervaded by the Divine. Take only what is necessary and do not covet another's wealth."

This verse teaches that money is not hoarded; it flows. If you serve well, provide genuine value, and operate with integrity, you will attract more than enough wealth.

Practical Mindset Shifts for Salespeople

1. **Believe in Value, Not Price:** Your product solves problems. If the value outweighs the cost, you should confidently charge what it's worth.

2. **Detach from Desperation:** People can sense desperation. Approach sales from a mindset of service, not need.
3. **Think Long-Term:** A small commission today is nothing compared to the lifetime value of a happy customer.

The Law of Attraction in Wealth Creation

Just as a magnet attracts metal, your thoughts, emotions, and actions attract money or repel it. This is why some people seem to make money effortlessly, while others struggle despite working hard.

Krishna confirms this in the Bhagavad Gita:

"मन्मना भव मद्भक्तो मद्याजी मां नमस्कुरु।
मामेवैष्यसि सत्यं ते प्रतिजाने प्रियोऽसि मे॥"
(Bhagavad Gita 18.65)

"Fix your mind on me, be devoted to me, and worship me with sincerity. When you align with the higher purpose, success follows naturally."

The same applies to money. If you focus on creating value, solving problems, and serving others, money will come to you. But if you chase money desperately, it will elude you.

The Vedic Perspective on Wealth Creation - How to Attract Wealth in Sales

The Vedas describe Lakshmi, the goddess of wealth, as fickle–she does not stay in one place unless certain virtues are cultivated. The ancient sages identified these virtues and provided clear guidance on how one can invite wealth into their lives.

One such timeless teaching comes from Subhashita Vachanani, which beautifully describes the qualities of a person upon whom Lakshmi (wealth) naturally bestows herself:

"उत्साह सम्पन्नं अधीर्घ सूत्रं क्रियाविधिज्ञं व्यसनेष्वासक्तं।
शूरं कृतज्ञं दृढ़सौहृदं च लक्ष्मीः स्वयं याति निवासहेतोः॥"

Utsaah sampannam Adheergha sutram kriya
vidhigyam vyasaneshva saktam
Shuram krutagyam Dhruda Souhrudam cha
lakshmeehi svyam yaati nivasa hetoho

Meaning:

"Wealth naturally resides with those who are enthusiastic, efficient, action-oriented, free from addictions, courageous, grateful, and deeply committed to strong relationships."

This verse serves as a powerful blueprint for attracting money in sales. Let's break it down and apply it to our profession.

---

1. Enthusiasm: The Magnet for Opportunities

उत्साह सम्पन्नं (Utsaah Sampannam) –
"Filled with enthusiasm"

Enthusiasm is the magnet that attracts opportunities. A salesperson who approaches prospects with genuine excitement and passion makes a lasting impression.

⚡ **Example:** A struggling insurance agent once asked his successful colleague, "*What's your secret?*" The response was simple:

"I love what I do, and people can feel it." Customers don't just buy products; they buy energy.

Sales Action Step:

- Approach every sales call with energy and optimism.
- Develop a morning ritual to boost enthusiasm—chanting, affirmations, or a power routine.

---

2. Efficiency and Speed: The Key to Closing More Deals

अधीर्घ सूत्रं (Adheergha Sutram) –
"Not delaying or procrastinating"

Sales is about momentum. The faster you move, the more deals you close. Procrastination is the enemy of financial success.

⚡ **Case Study:** Two salespeople receive a high-potential lead. One follows up immediately and schedules a meeting. The other waits a few days, thinking, *"I'll reach out later."* The first one closes the deal while the second loses the opportunity.

Sales Action Step:

- Speed up your response time.
- Don't overanalyze—take action immediately.

---

3. Mastery of Sales Skills

क्रियाविधिज्ञं (Kriya Vidhigyam) –
"Expert in execution and process"

Success in sales is not just about hard work but smart work. A Rainmaker salesperson masters the art of selling—from prospecting to closing.

⚡ **Example from the Mahabharata:** Arjuna wasn't just skilled in archery; he trained rigorously under Guru Dronacharya. His mastery set him apart.

Sales Action Step:

- Keep refining your skills. Learn. Practice. Apply.
- Invest in books, training, and mentorship.

---

4. Self-Control and Financial Discipline

व्यासनेष्वासक्तं (Vyasaneṣhva Asaktam) –
"Free from bad habits and addictions"

Many salespeople make money but lose it just as fast due to poor financial discipline. **The**

Bhagavad Gita (6.16) warns:

"नात्यश्नतस्तु योगोऽस्ति न चैकान्तमनश्नतः।
न चातिस्वप्नशीलस्य जाग्रतो नैव चार्जुन॥"

"There is no success for one who eats too much or too little, who sleeps too much or too little."

⚡ **Practical Tip:** Avoid unnecessary spending. Reinvest earnings into self-growth, savings, and investments.

---

5. Courage and Risk-Taking in Sales

शूरं (Shuram) –
"Courageous and bold"

A Rainmaker salesperson takes calculated risks. They don't wait for perfect conditions but act despite fear.

⚡ **Example from Ramayana:** When Hanuman was asked to cross the ocean to reach Lanka, he didn't hesitate. His faith and courage made the impossible possible.

Sales Action Step:

- Take bold action.
- Make that difficult call.
- Approach that high-value client.

---

6. Gratitude – The Secret to Abundance

कृतज्ञं (Krutagyam) –
"Grateful and appreciative"

Gratitude is a wealth magnet. The more you appreciate what you have, the more you receive.

Sales Action Step:

- Keep a gratitude journal—write three things you're grateful for daily.
- Thank customers, even if they don't buy. Relationships matter.

7. Strong Relationships Build Wealth

दृढ़सौहृदं (Dhruda Souhrudam) –
"Having strong, lasting relationships"

The biggest asset in sales isn't money–it's trust and relationships. Wealth follows those who build strong connections.

⚡ **Real-Life Example:** Warren Buffett, one of the world's richest people, emphasizes relationships over profits. He once said, "*The best investment you can make is in your network.*"

Sales Action Step:

- Build genuine relationships.
- Focus on helping, not just selling.

Applying This Wisdom in Sales

These aren't just abstract concepts but **practical success traits** that can be developed.

- **Be enthusiastic about what you sell.** Customers can sense energy, and they buy from those who believe in their product.
- **Avoid laziness–take immediate action.** Wealth flows to those who seize opportunities instead of waiting for the "perfect time."
- **Master your craft–learn sales psychology, negotiation, and customer needs.** The more you know, the more valuable you become.

- **Avoid distractions and unethical shortcuts.** Focus on building genuine, lasting success.
- **Take bold action.** Ask for the sale, make that call, and push beyond fear.
- **Practice gratitude.** A grateful heart attracts more opportunities.
- **Build trust and relationships.** People do business with those they trust, and repeat business is more valuable than one-time sales.

When we embody these principles, wealth doesn't just come to us—we become a magnet for wealth.

As Krishna says in the **Bhagavad Gita** (9.22):

"अनन्याश्चिन्तयन्तो मां ये जनाः पर्युपासते।
तेषां नित्याभियुक्तानां योगक्षेमं वहाम्यहम्॥"

"*For those who are steadfast in devotion, I personally ensure their prosperity and protection.*"

Money as a Form of Energy Exchange

In ancient times, trade wasn't just about money—it was an exchange of karma. The Vedic system believed that the way you earn and spend money affects your future prosperity. If you earn dishonestly or hoard money, you create negative karma. But if you earn with integrity and use wealth for good, prosperity flows effortlessly.

The Mahabharata teaches this through the character of Karna. He was known as Daanveer (the Generous One) because he gave without hesitation. Though he faced hardships, his name is still remembered with reverence.

Krishna reminds us in the Gita:

"त्यक्त्वा कर्मफलासङ्गं नित्यतृप्तो निराश्रयः ।
कर्मण्यभिप्रवृत्तोऽपि नैव किञ्चित्करोति सः ॥"
(Bhagavad Gita 4.20)

"One who performs work without attachment to the results remains content and free, regardless of external circumstances."

What This Means for Salespeople

- Sell with integrity, and your reputation will bring you long-term wealth.
- Never pressure customers into a sale; guide them toward the right decision.
- Detach from commissions and focus on relationships—money follows trust.

Overcoming Limiting Beliefs About Wealth

Many people subconsciously fear wealth. They believe:

- "Rich people are greedy."
- "Money changes people."
- "If I earn too much, I'll lose my spiritual path."

But Hindu scriptures never condemn wealthMoney is not just about numbers in your bank account—it is energy, karma, and an extension of your service to the world.

By embracing an abundance mindset, focusing on service, and following ancient wisdom, you will naturally attract prosperity in sales and life.

—they only warn against greed. Lakshmi stays where dharma (righteousness) is followed.

Krishna states:

"काङ्क्षन्तः कर्मणां सिद्धिं यजन्त इह देवताः।
क्षिप्रं हि मानुषे लोके सिद्धिर्भवति कर्मजा॥"
(Bhagavad Gita 4.12)

"Those who seek success in their actions worship with sincerity. And success comes quickly to those who work diligently."

How to Develop a Wealth-Accepting Mindset

1. **See Money as a Tool, Not a Goal** – Use it to grow, serve, and expand opportunities.
2. **Visualize Your Ideal Financial Future** – Picture yourself earning with integrity and using money wisely.
3. **Affirmations for Abundance** – Repeat: *"I provide value, and wealth flows effortlessly to me."*
4. **Gratitude Rituals** – Every morning, thank the universe for what you already have. This shifts your mind from scarcity to abundance.
5. **Offer Genuine Service** – Approach sales as a way to serve, not as a transaction.
6. **Give Before You Receive** – In ancient India, kings and merchants donated before starting new ventures. Help someone in need, and prosperity will return manifold.
7. **Set Intentions, Not Just Goals** – Instead of just setting a revenue target, set an intention like, *"I will help 50 people solve a problem this month."* Money will follow naturally.

Conclusion: Becoming a Wealth Magnet

Money is not just about numbers in your bank account–it is energy, karma, and an extension of your service to the world.

By embracing an abundance mindset, focusing on service, and following ancient wisdom, you will naturally attract prosperity in sales and life.

Krishna's final lesson on wealth:

"अनन्याश्चिन्तयन्तो मां ये जनाः पर्युपासते।
तेषां नित्याभियुक्तानां योगक्षेमं वहाम्यहम्॥"
(Bhagavad Gita 9.22)

The Bhagavad Gita (9.22) promises:

"योगक्षेमं वहाम्यहम्"

"For those who walk the righteous path, I personally ensure their prosperity."

Walk this path, and wealth will not only follow–it will **stay**.

"Those who think of me with single-minded focus and devotion, I take care of their needs and ensure their well-being."

The message is simple–focus on service, trust, and integrity, and wealth will follow effortlessly.

Chapter 15

Mastering Follow-Ups – The Lost Art of Persistence

"A river cuts through rock, not because of its power, but because of its persistence."

"Success in sales is not about making the first contact; it is about staying in the game long enough to win the trust of your prospect."

Most salespeople believe that closing a deal is all about delivering the perfect pitch. But the truth is, a great pitch alone rarely seals the deal. The real battle is fought in the follow-up stage. According to research, 80% of sales require at least five follow-ups after the initial meeting, yet 44% of salespeople give up after just one follow-up.

Why? Because they fear being seen as pushy.

But history and ancient wisdom teach us that persistence is the key to success. Those who master the art of follow-up—without being aggressive—reap the rewards.

A lack of persistence and strategic follow-ups leads to lost deals.

To truly master follow-ups, we must embrace the wisdom of perseverance—as exemplified in the story of **King Bhagirath's quest to bring the Ganga to Earth.**

The Power of Perseverance – Bhagirath's Determination to Bring Ganga to Earth

The story of Bhagirath in Hindu mythology is a powerful lesson in perseverance.

King Bhagirath had a mission: to bring the divine river Ganga from heaven to earth to cleanse his ancestors' sins. But this was not an easy task.

- He performed penance for 1000 years to please Brahma, who finally granted his wish.
- But Brahma warned that Ganga's force would destroy the earth.
- Bhagirath then performed another long penance to please Lord Shiva, who finally tamed Ganga in his locks.

Even after this, Bhagirath had to guide Ganga through many obstacles before she finally reached her destination.

Sales Follow-Up Lesson: Like Bhagirath, you must be:

✅ Patient and Persistent – Deals take time.

✅ Flexible in Approach – Adapt when obstacles arise.

✅ Committed to the Goal – Stay focused despite setbacks.

The same principle applies to follow-ups in sales.

Bhagavad Gita on Perseverance in Action

"न हि कश्चित् क्षणमपि जातु तिष्ठत्यकर्मकृत् |
कार्यते ह्यवशः कर्म सर्वः प्रकृतिजैर्गुणैः ||"
(Bhagavad Gita 3.5)

"No one can remain without action even for a moment; everyone is driven to act by their inherent qualities."

This verse teaches us that continuous action is the key to success—a principle that applies directly to sales follow-ups.

Sales Lesson: Like Bhagirath, successful salespeople understand that the deal is won through persistence—not just the first pitch.

Why Most Salespeople Lose Deals in the Follow-Up Stage

Salespeople often struggle with follow-ups for three main reasons:

1. **Fear of Rejection** – They assume that a lack of immediate response means the prospect isn't interested. In reality, most prospects need time to make a decision.
2. **Lack of a Follow-Up System** – Many salespeople follow up inconsistently, which makes them forgettable.
3. **Failure to Add Value** – Follow-ups that only push for a sale get ignored. Effective follow-ups build trust and provide value.

The great sage Chanakya once said:

"धैर्यं परमो लाभः" (Dhairyam Paramo Labhah)
"Patience is the greatest gain."

If you persist with patience and strategy, you will outlast the competition.

The Psychology Behind Why Prospects Delay Decisions

Before we dive into advanced follow-up strategies, let's understand why prospects don't respond immediately.

1. Decision Fatigue

Leaders and business owners make hundreds of decisions daily. Your offer is just one of many competing for their attention.

✅ **Follow-Up Strategy:** Simplify decisions with concise, high-impact messages.

◈ Example: Instead of saying, "Can we schedule a meeting?", try:

☞ "I can share a 2-minute voice note summarizing the key benefits–would that work?"

2. Loss Aversion Bias

People fear losing something more than they desire gaining something. Your follow-ups must emphasize potential loss if they delay.

✅ **Follow-Up Strategy:** Show what they might lose if they delay.

◈ Example: Instead of saying, "This plan offers great returns", try:

👉 "Every month you delay, you miss out on potential gains of ₹X–here's a case study of someone who took action."

Timeless Sales Wisdom from the Ramayana - Hanuman's Relentless Pursuit

In the Ramayana, Hanuman demonstrates unmatched persistence when searching for Sita in Lanka. Despite facing:

✔ Demonic obstacles (guardians of Lanka)

✔ Self-doubt (momentary hesitation)

✔ Ravana's threats

He never stopped until he successfully found Sita and delivered Lord Rama's message.

Ancient Wisdom on Unstoppable Effort

"न हि सुप्तस्य सिंहस्य प्रविशन्ति मुखे मृगाः |"
(Hitopadesha – Ancient Indian Wisdom Text)

"Even a lion will not have food fall into its mouth while sleeping."

💡 Sales Lesson: Just like Hanuman, a salesperson must overcome objections and rejections with an unwavering follow-up strategy.

Strategies to Follow Up Effectively Without Being Pushy

1. Follow the Rule of Seven (Sapta-Samudra Nyaya)

In the Vedic tradition, the number seven is considered sacred. Seven oceans, seven continents, seven days of the week–many natural cycles follow this pattern.

In sales, the "Rule of Seven" states that a prospect needs to see or hear about your product at least seven times before making a purchase decision.

Sales Action Plan:

- Don't give up after one or two follow-ups. Commit to at least seven meaningful touchpoints.
- Spread your follow-ups over multiple channels—calls, emails, messages, social media, and personal visits.

2. Timing is Everything – The Kautilya Approach

Chanakya (Kautilya), the brilliant strategist, emphasized *kaalajnaana* (timing intelligence) in Arthashastra. He believed that even the best strategies would fail if applied at the wrong time.

How to Apply in Sales:

- Follow up when your prospect is most receptive. Morning hours or post-lunch are generally best.
- If a prospect says, "Call me next week," respect their request but be specific—ask for a date and time.
- Track prospect behavior. If they opened your email but didn't reply, follow up with additional insights rather than asking, "Did you see my email?"

3. Use Storytelling (The Panchatantra Technique)

The Panchatantra, India's timeless collection of moral stories, teaches us that people remember stories better than facts. Instead of sending a generic follow-up message, share a relevant customer success story.

⚡ **Example:** If you're selling insurance, instead of just saying, *"Have you thought more about the policy?"*, share a short story:

"A client recently hesitated to buy life insurance but later regretted waiting when an emergency hit. Thankfully, he had a small policy in place, which provided financial relief. I wanted to share this with you because your financial security matters, and I'd love to help you make the right decision."

Stories engage emotions, making your follow-up more compelling.

4. The "Give Before You Ask" Strategy – The Dakshina Principle

In ancient India, before a disciple asked the guru for wisdom, they first offered *dakshina* (a token of gratitude or service). This principle teaches us that giving comes before receiving.

Sales Application:

- Before asking your prospect to buy, give them something valuable.
- This could be a helpful article, industry insights, a product demo, or a free consultation.

This builds trust, making them more likely to engage with you.

5. The Krishna Approach – Personalization and Adaptability

In the Bhagavad Gita, Krishna didn't give Arjuna a one-size-fits-all lesson. Instead, he adapted his message based on Arjuna's emotions and concerns.

Similarly, your follow-ups should be tailored to your prospect's unique needs.

How to Apply:

- Instead of generic messages, reference something specific from your last conversation.
- Use their name often–it personalizes the interaction.
- Adapt your tone. If they are analytical, give logical reasons. If they are emotional, appeal to their values.

6. Detachment from the Outcome – The Gita's Sales Mantra

Krishna's core teaching in the Bhagavad Gita (2.47) is:

"कर्मण्येवाधिकारस्ते मा फलेषु कदाचन।"

"You have the right to perform your duty, but not to the fruits of your action."

In sales, this means focusing on the process of follow-ups rather than obsessing over immediate results.

Sales Action Plan:

- Follow up consistently without attachment to whether the client buys today or next month.
- Your goal is to serve, educate, and be top-of-mind when they are ready to decide.

The Follow-Up Blueprint – A Practical Plan

1. **First Follow-Up (Within 24-48 Hours)** – A simple thank-you message with a key takeaway from your discussion.
2. **Second Follow-Up (3-5 Days Later)** – Provide additional value, like a relevant article, case study, or product demo.

3. **Third Follow-Up (7-10 Days Later)** – Address common objections they might have.
4. **Fourth Follow-Up (2 Weeks Later)** – Use a success story or testimonial to reinforce trust.
5. **Fifth Follow-Up (One Month Later)** – Check-in with a personal message: *"I was thinking about our last discussion and wanted to see how things are progressing on your end."*
6. **Sixth Follow-Up (3-6 Months Later)** – If they haven't converted, reconnect in a non-sales way—maybe by sharing an industry update.
7. **Final Follow-Up (1 Year Later)** – If they still haven't bought, reach out with a special offer or new opportunity.

The Five Types of Follow-Ups Every Salesperson Must Master

1. The Reminder Follow-Up (Gentle Check-In)

◈ Purpose: Keep your proposal top of mind without sounding pushy.

◈ Best Used: 2–3 days after the first meeting.

◈ Example: ☞ *"Hi [Prospect's Name], just checking in on our last discussion. Let me know if you need any clarifications!"*

---

2. The Value-Added Follow-Up (Educate & Engage)

◈ Purpose: Keep the prospect engaged by adding value rather than just asking for updates.

◈ Best Used: 5–7 days after the last interaction.

◈ Example: ☞ *"I came across this article on [industry trend] and thought you'd find it useful–sharing it here."*

---

3. The Scarcity Follow-Up (Creating Urgency)

◈ Purpose: Encourage faster decision-making using FOMO (Fear of Missing Out).

◈ Best Used: When the prospect is indecisive.

◈ Example: ☞ *"Just letting you know–only 3 spots left for this offer. Let me know if you'd like me to reserve one for you."*

---

4. The Social Proof Follow-Up (Building Trust)

◈ Purpose: Address hesitation by showcasing real-world success stories.

◈ Best Used: When prospects express doubt.

◈ Example: ☞ *"One of our clients faced the same challenge you mentioned. They used our solution and saw [result]. Would you like me to connect you with them?"*

---

5. The Last-Resort Follow-Up (Final Attempt Before Closing File)

◈ Purpose: Politely push for a decision without sounding desperate.

◈ Best Used: When the prospect has gone cold after multiple follow-ups.

◈ Example: ☞ *"I understand you're busy. I don't want to keep bothering you, so unless I hear otherwise, I'll assume this isn't a priority right now. Feel free to reach out if things change."*

Case Study – How Smart Follow-Ups Closed a ₹5 Crore Deal

Arjun, an insurance advisor, was pitching a ₹5 crore term insurance plan to a business owner, Amit.

Stage 1 – Initial Meeting
Amit showed interest but said, *"Let me think about it."*

Stage 2 – First Follow-Up (No Response)
Arjun sent a gentle check-in message after 3 days—Amit didn't reply.

Stage 3 – Second Follow-Up (Still No Response)
Arjun shared a short video case study. Still no reply.

Stage 4 – Third Follow-Up (FOMO Trigger – Amit Responds!)

Arjun sent: ☞ "Amit, I recently worked with a similar business owner. He postponed his insurance, and six months later, his premiums tripled due to health issues. I don't want you to face the same risk."

✅ Result: Amit replied, *"Let's meet again."*

Conclusion – Follow-Up Like a Rainmaker

Mastering follow-ups is not about persistence alone—it's about *smart* persistence. By applying the lessons of Bhagirath, Krishna, Chanakya, and the great texts of India, you can build relationships that lead to sales success.

The biggest mistake in sales isn't losing a deal—it's giving up too soon.

🚀 Key Takeaways:

✔ Follow-ups should be persistent, not pushy.

✔ Use psychology to drive urgency.

✔ Leverage stories, testimonials, and FOMO.

✔ Be like Bhagirath—stay committed until you succeed!

Bhagavad Gita's Final Wisdom on Follow-Ups

"योगस्थः कुरु कर्माणि सङ्गं त्यक्त्वा धनञ्जय |
सिद्ध्यसिद्ध्योः समो भूत्वा समत्वं योग उच्यते ||"
(Bhagavad Gita 2.48)

"Remain steadfast in action, without attachment to success or failure—this equanimity is yoga."

💡 Sales Lesson: Follow-ups must be consistent and detached from immediate results—because perseverance always wins in the end!

Chapter 16

The Spiritual Psychology of Persuasion – How to Speak to the Subconscious Mind

Introduction: The Power of Words in Sales

Words are not just sounds; they are vibrations that shape reality. Ancient sages in India understood this and used specific words, mantras, and affirmations to influence the minds of their disciples and kings.

As a salesperson, your words have the power to inspire, persuade, and transform a prospect's decision-making process. But most salespeople focus only on logical arguments, ignoring the subconscious—where real decisions are made.

In this chapter, we'll uncover how ancient wisdom teaches us to speak directly to the subconscious mind, using the principles of mantras, affirmations, and storytelling to create irresistible sales pitches.

1. The Power of Words in Ancient Scriptures

The Vedas, Upanishads, and Bhagavad Gita emphasize that words have the power to shape reality. The sound of a word carries a vibration that penetrates the subconscious mind and influences thoughts, emotions, and decisions.

Example from the Bhagavad Gita

In the Bhagavad Gita (17.15), Lord Krishna explains the threefold discipline of speech:

"अनुद्वेगकरं वाक्यं सत्यं प्रियं हितं च यत्।
स्वाध्यायाभ्यसनं चैव वाङ्मयं तप उच्यते॥"

"Anudvegakaram vaakyam satyam priyam hitam cha yat,
Swadhyayabhyasanam chaiva vaangmayam tapa uchyate."

Translation: Speech that does not cause distress, that is truthful, pleasant, and beneficial, and that involves the regular recitation of scriptures—such speech is considered a form of austerity.

Sales Takeaway:

- Your words should be truthful (authentic sales pitches),
- Pleasant (engaging and positive tone), and
- Beneficial (adding value to the customer's life).

---

2. The Science of Mantras and Affirmations in Sales

How Mantras Work in the Mind

A mantra is a carefully crafted combination of sounds that bypass the logical mind and influence the subconscious. This is why repetition of mantras brings transformation.

Similarly, in sales, when you repeat the right words with confidence and clarity, you can plant the right thoughts in the prospect's mind.

Example 1: The Power of a Persuasive Opening Line

A top-performing insurance agent once experimented with two different ways to start his client meetings.

- First Approach (Ordinary): "Sir, I wanted to discuss an insurance policy with you."
- Second Approach (Persuasive): "Sir, imagine if your family never has to worry about financial security, no matter what happens. Let me show you how to make that a reality."

Guess which approach worked better? The second one!

Why? Because the second approach painted a vivid picture in the subconscious mind of the prospect.

How Rishis Framed Their Words

In the Upanishads, wisdom was often shared in a way that invited imagination and created mental images.

For example, the Mundaka Upanishad gives this metaphor:

"द्वा सुपर्णा सयुजा सखाया
समानं वृक्षं परिषस्वजाते। "

"Two birds, inseparable companions, perch on the same tree. One eats the sweet fruit, while the other simply watches."

This metaphor represents the soul and the body. The soul is the observer, while the body engages in worldly activities.

Sales Takeaway:

- Instead of listing product features, use powerful imagery in your pitch.
- Make the prospect "see" the benefits instead of just hearing them.

In ancient India, sages used powerful speech techniques to transform people's beliefs and behaviors. Here are two examples that we can apply to sales:

Example 1: Krishna's Persuasive Speech to Arjuna

When Arjuna was paralyzed by doubt on the battlefield, Krishna didn't use logic alone. He used a blend of storytelling, affirmations, and authority to change Arjuna's mindset.

He said in the Bhagavad Gita (2.3):

"क्लैब्यं मा स्म गमः पार्थ नैतत्त्वय्युपपद्यते।
क्षुद्रं हृदयदौर्बल्यं त्यक्त्वोत्तिष्ठ परंतप॥"

(Klaibyam Ma Smagamah Partha Naitat Tvayyupapadyate,
Kshudram Hridaya Daurbalyam Tyaktvottishta Parantapa)

Meaning:
"Do not yield to weakness, O Arjuna! It does not suit you. Cast off this petty faint-heartedness and arise like a warrior."

⚡ **Sales Lesson:**
Prospects often hesitate due to fear or doubt. A great salesperson, like Krishna, reminds them of their own strength and helps them move forward confidently.

Instead of saying:
"You should buy this insurance policy because it has good benefits."

Say:
"You've worked hard to build a secure future. This plan is a shield that ensures your family's safety, no matter what. You deserve that peace of mind."

Example 2: The Ramayana - The Power of a Single Word

When Lord Hanuman was sent to find Sita in Lanka, she was depressed and hopeless in Ashok Vatika. Hanuman didn't start by listing Rama's achievements or logical arguments.

Instead, he uttered just one word—"राम" (Rama).

That single word instantly changed Sita's emotions. She knew Hanuman was a messenger of truth and felt reassured.

⚡ **Sales Lesson:** One powerful word can change everything in a conversation. Words like:

✔ "Security" (for insurance)

✔ "Growth" (for investments)

✔ "Freedom" (for financial planning)

These words speak directly to the subconscious mind and create instant trust.

---

3. Crafting Irresistible Sales Pitches Using Ancient Wisdom

A great sales pitch is not just about features and benefits. It should follow the timeless formula of persuasion:

☑ **Mantra (**Memorable Message**)**

☑ **Story (**Emotional Connection**)**

☑ **Affirmation (**Positive Reinforcement)

Step 1: Start with a Powerful "Mantra"

Ancient mantras worked because they were:

✔ Short (Easy to remember)

✔ Rhythmic (Pleasant to hear)

✔ Emotionally Charged (Create strong feelings)

Sales Example:

Instead of saying:
"This mutual fund has great returns."

Say:
"This is not just a mutual fund. It's your future, growing safely every single day."

The subconscious mind loves certainty. When your words create a strong belief, the prospect naturally leans toward a yes.

Step 2: Use a Story to Create Emotional Connection

People buy with emotion, then justify with logic.

◈ Example:
If you're selling insurance, don't just say,
"Insurance protects your family."

Tell a story:
"A father once thought he had years to save. But life is uncertain.

His small investment in insurance became his family's lifeline when he was no longer around. The question is—who do you want to protect?"

This approach activates the subconscious mind and makes the prospect feel the urgency of taking action.

Step 3: Reinforce the Message with Affirmations

Ancient sages used affirmations to rewire minds.

In sales, you can use this technique to strengthen a prospect's decision:

✔ "I deserve a secure future for my family."

✔ "I am making a wise decision for long-term wealth."

✔ "I take smart financial actions today for a stress-free tomorrow."

When a prospect repeats affirmations, they subconsciously convince themselves to buy.

---

4. How to Speak Directly to the Subconscious Mind

Most people make decisions emotionally and then justify them logically. The subconscious mind is influenced by:

- Repetition (Hearing something multiple times builds belief)
- Emotional words (Feelings create stronger memories than facts)
- Authority and credibility (We trust experts and leaders)

Example 1: Krishna's Persuasion of Arjuna – Speaking to the Subconscious Mind

In the Mahabharata, Arjuna hesitates before the great Kurukshetra war. His conscious mind is filled with doubt, emotions, and fear. Instead of commanding Arjuna to fight, Krishna awakens his subconscious wisdom using:

✔ Powerful metaphors (comparing life to a battlefield).

✔ Deep psychological triggers (duty, honor, and eternal truth).

✔ Reframing fear into clarity and confidence.

the Bhagavad Gita (2.47)

"कर्मण्येवाधिकारस्ते मा फलेषु कदाचन |
मा कर्मफलहेतुर्भूर्मा ते सङ्गोऽस्त्वकर्मणि ||"
(Bhagavad Gita 2.47)

"You have the right to perform your duty, but never to the results. Do not be attached to the fruits of your actions, nor be inclined towards inaction."

◈ **Sales Lesson:** When a prospect hesitates, they fear making the wrong decision. Instead of arguing with logic, reframe their perspective:

💡 **Instead of saying:** "This plan is great, trust me."

☞ Say: "Like a warrior who must act without fear of outcome, making the right financial decision is about taking action–not overanalyzing the results."

By shifting focus to action over hesitation, Krishna removed Arjuna's fear, just as a sales leader removes a client's doubts.

Example 2: Vashishtha vs. Vishwamitra – The Power of Persuasion Over Force

Sage Vashishtha and King Vishwamitra had a famous conflict over divine power. Vishwamitra, despite being a great king, initially relied on brute force to achieve his goals, while Vashishtha used the power of speech and wisdom to overcome obstacles.

At one point, Vishwamitra attacked Vashishtha, but instead of retaliating, Vashishtha calmly used the power of his words to neutralize the aggression.

Ramayana (Balakanda 1.57.20)

"नास्ति तपसम् साम्यं शस्त्राणां चापि विद्यते |
तपसा क्षीयते सर्वं नास्ति तपसम् बलं परम् ||"
(Ramayana – Balakanda 1.57.20)

"There is no power equal to wisdom and self-discipline. All weapons can be neutralized through the power of self-restraint. There is no strength greater than wisdom."

◆ **Sales Lesson:** Many salespeople push too hard, trying to force a decision. This creates resistance.

💡 Instead of saying: "You must buy this now, or you'll regret it."

👉 Say: "Great decisions are made with clarity, not pressure. Let's look at how this fits into your goals."

By using calm confidence instead of pressure, Vashishtha defeated Vishwamitra's force. Similarly, in sales, true persuasion comes from wisdom, patience, and guiding the prospect's mind—rather than forcing a sale.

Case Study: Apple's Marketing Genius

Steve Jobs understood subconscious persuasion better than anyone. When launching the first iPod, he didn't say:

"This device has 5GB of storage."

Instead, he said:

"1,000 songs in your pocket."

See the difference? Instead of facts, he used an image and an emotional hook.

Sales Takeaway:

- Avoid technical jargon.
- Use simple, emotional language that the prospect's mind can visualize.

5. The Ancient Art of Closing Deals with Silence

In Indian philosophy, silence is considered as powerful as words. **The Yoga Sutras of Patanjali emphasize:**

"योगश्चित्तवृत्तिनिरोधः"

"Yoga is the cessation of mental chatter."

Sometimes, the best persuasion technique is silence. After making a strong sales pitch, instead of over-explaining, try pausing and letting the prospect process your words.

Example: The Power of Silence in Sales

A successful life insurance salesperson once said:

"After I present my pitch, I stay silent for 10 seconds. In those 10 seconds, the prospect either accepts the idea or asks me a question. Either way, I win."

Sales Takeaway:

- Make your pitch, then pause.
- Let the prospect's mind do the persuasion.

Conclusion: The Subconscious Path to Sales Mastery

A true Rainmaker salesperson doesn't sell–they guide the prospect's mind toward an inevitable "yes."

✔ Speak with conviction (Your words create reality)

✔ Use emotional storytelling (Logic alone won't convince)

✔ Reinforce with affirmations (Prospects must believe they are making a great choice)

When you master the psychology of persuasion, sales stops feeling like selling. Instead, it becomes a natural flow–like a mantra that transforms lives.

✅ Final Action Step: Try using one mantra, story, or affirmation in your next sales pitch and watch the magic unfold.

Chapter 17

Tapasya in Sales – The Power of Perseverance and Self-Discipline

"Success in sales, like in life, is not about luck–it is about discipline, perseverance, and unwavering commitment to the process. Just as a sage perfects his sadhana through tapasya, a salesperson achieves greatness through relentless effort and self-discipline."

The Meaning of Tapasya in Sales

The word Tapasya (तपस्या) originates from the Sanskrit root 'Tap' (तप्), which means to heat, to undergo penance, or to practice intense discipline to achieve mastery. In the context of sales, Tapasya represents dedication, effort, and the willingness to endure discomfort for a greater reward.

Sales is not a profession for the faint-hearted. It demands resilience in the face of rejection, patience in the face of delays, and continuous self-improvement. The difference between an average salesperson and a Rainmaker is **Tapasya–their ability to persist through challenges with unwavering faith and discipline.**

Just as a yogi sits in deep meditation despite external distractions, a great salesperson stays committed to their goals despite objections, failed deals, and rejections.

---

1. The Discipline of Tapasya – Learning from the Rishis

The ancient rishis (sages) practiced extreme discipline, dedicating their lives to meditation, scriptural study, and deep inquiry. Their tapasya wasn't just about suffering—it was about **consistency, focus, and detachment from distractions.**

A salesperson must adopt the same approach. Mastery in sales comes from relentless **practice, preparation, and performance.**

Bhagavad Gita on Discipline in Work

Krishna emphasizes the power of disciplined action:

"योगस्थः कुरु कर्माणि संगं त्यक्त्वा धनंजय।
सिद्ध्यसिद्ध्योः समो भूत्वा समत्वं योग उच्यते॥"

yoga-sthaḥ kuru karmāṇi saṅgaṁ tyaktvā dhanañjaya
siddhy-asiddhyoḥ samo bhūtvā samatvaṁ yoga uchyate
(Bhagavad Gita 2.48)

"Be steadfast in the performance of your duty, O Arjuna, abandoning attachment to success and failure. Such equanimity is called yoga."

A true salesperson must follow this philosophy—focus on the process rather than being attached to immediate results.

---

2. Arjuna's Tapasya – The Power of Unwavering Focus

Arjuna, the greatest archer of his time, became who he was because of his **Tapasya—his single-minded focus and relentless practice.**

One day, Guru Dronacharya placed a wooden bird on a tree and asked his students to aim for its eye. Before allowing them to shoot, he asked what they saw.

- Yudhishthira said, "I see the tree, the branches, and the bird."
- Bhima said, "I see the bird and the sky behind it."
- Duryodhana said, "I see the entire bird, the tree, and everything around it."

Finally, Dronacharya turned to Arjuna and asked, **"What do you see?"**

Arjuna replied, "I see only the eye of the bird. Nothing else."

Dronacharya smiled and said, **"Shoot!"** Arjuna hit the target perfectly.

Lesson for Salespeople:

Like Arjuna, a Rainmaker must develop laser focus. If you start your day thinking about ten different things, you'll never hit your target. If you focus only on your goal—**closing deals, building relationships, and mastering your craft**—success becomes inevitable.

---

3. Ramayana – Hanuman's Tapasya and Unstoppable Willpower

Hanuman is a legendary example of **Tapasya in action.**

When tasked with finding Sita, he faced an impossible journey. He had to:

- Cross the vast ocean
- Battle powerful demons
- Search through Lanka
- Overcome countless obstacles

Did he hesitate? No. His **faith, discipline, and perseverance** made the impossible possible.

Bhagavad Gita on Perseverance

Krishna teaches in the Bhagavad Gita:

"न हि कश्चित्क्षणमपि जातु तिष्ठत्यकर्मकृत्।
कार्यते ह्यवशः कर्म सर्वः प्रकृतिजैर्गुणैः॥"

na hi kaścit kṣaṇam api jātu tiṣṭhatyakarma-kṛt
kāryate hyavaśaḥ karma sarvaḥ prakṛiti-jair guṇaiḥ
(Bhagavad Gita 3.5)

"No one can remain inactive even for a moment. Everyone is forced to act according to their nature."

Lesson for Salespeople:

Success in sales, like Hanuman's mission, requires action. Make the calls, do the follow-ups, meet the clients—every single day.

---

4. The Science of Repetition – Why Daily Practice Matters

Ancient rituals like Sandhya Vandana (morning prayers) and Agnihotra (fire offerings) were performed daily. Why? Because repetition creates mastery.

In sales, the same principle applies: **Repetition builds excellence.**

- Daily Sales Calls → Improves Communication
- Daily Product Study → Enhances Confidence
- Daily Objection Handling Practice → Strengthens Negotiation Skills

Atharva Veda on Hard Work

"न कश्चित् सुव्रतो भवति यावत् त्वं तपसा न याति।"
(Atharva Veda 12.1.12)

"No one becomes great without consistent effort and tapasya."

A salesperson must adopt this principle—train daily, improve daily, grow daily.

---

5. The Power of Patience – Learning from the Bamboo Tree

The Chinese Bamboo tree takes **five years** to grow underground before it sprouts. But once it emerges, it grows **90 feet in just six weeks!**

Most salespeople quit too soon, expecting quick results. But a Rainmaker understands that success is like the bamboo tree—it takes time, patience, and consistency before massive growth happens.

Bhagavad Gita on Patience and Steady Growth

"श्रेयान् स्वधर्मो विगुणः परधर्मात्स्वनुष्ठितात्।
स्वधर्मे निधनं श्रेयः परधर्मो भयावहः ॥"

śhreyān swa-dharmo viguṇaḥ para-dharmāt svanuṣhṭhitāt
swa-dharme nidhanaṁ śhreyaḥ para-dharmo bhayāvahaḥ
(Bhagavad Gita 3.35)

"It is better to follow your own path, even imperfectly, than to imitate another's path perfectly."

---

6. Creating a Tapasya-Driven Sales Routine

A Rainmaker follows a **disciplined daily routine** just like an ancient sage. Here's a **Tapasya-based Sales Routine** for unstoppable success:

Morning Routine (Prepare the Mind)

✔ Read scriptures (Gita, Upanishads, self-development books)

✔ Meditate for 5 minutes (clarity and focus)

✔ Visualize success (see yourself closing deals)

Midday Routine (Action Time)

✔ Make 20 sales calls

✔ Follow up with 10 prospects

✔ Send personalized messages

Evening Routine (Sharpen the Sword)

✔ Reflect on the day's successes & failures

✔ Learn a new skill (sales techniques, negotiation, persuasion)

✔ Plan for the next day

Conclusion: The Tapasya of a Rainmaker

A Rainmaker understands that Tapasya is the key to mastery.

- Like Arjuna, develop laser focus.
- Like Hanuman, cultivate unwavering willpower.
- Like the sages, practice daily discipline.

Krishna's final lesson on Tapasya:

"मन्मना भव मद्भक्तो मद्याजी मां नमस्कुरु।
मामेवैष्यसि सत्यं ते प्रतिजाने प्रियोऽसि मे॥"
(Bhagavad Gita 18.65)

"Dedicate yourself with faith, perseverance, and self-discipline, and success will be yours."

Now, take action. Your Tapasya begins today.

Chapter 18

The Inner Game – Mastering the Mind Before the Market

"The greatest distance between failure and success is the space between your ears."

Introduction: The Hidden Battlefield

Success in sales doesn't start with the client–it starts with the **mindset**. Every salesperson faces rejection, objections, pressure, and self-doubt. But the most powerful tool they have isn't a script, a CRM, or even their product. It's the ability to manage their thoughts and emotions under pressure.

This is the real inner game. Mastering it separates the average from the elite. And this truth is timeless–revealed in the Bhagavad Gita, where Arjuna, the mightiest of warriors, crumbles–not from fear of arrows, but from an overwhelmed mind.

Arjuna's Breakdown: When Mind Overpowers Muscle

Even a highly trained warrior like Arjuna was paralyzed when he saw his own family across the battlefield.

"दृष्ट्वेमं स्वजनं कृष्ण युयुत्सुं समुपस्थितम् || 28||
सीदन्ति मम गात्राणि मुखं च परिशुष्यति |"
(Bhagavad Gita 1.28)

"Seeing my own people arrayed for battle, my limbs give way and my mouth dries up."

"वेपथुश्च शरीरे मे रोमहर्षश्च जायते || 29||
गाण्डीवं स्रंसते हस्तात्त्वक्चैव परिदह्यते |"

"My body shudders, my hair stands on end, my bow slips from my hand, and my skin burns."

"न च शक्नोम्यवस्थातुं भ्रमतीव च मे मनः || 30||
निमित्तानि च पश्यामि विपरीतानि केशव |"

"I cannot stand still, my mind is in confusion, and I see inauspicious signs all around."

"न च श्रेयोऽनुपश्यामि हत्वा स्वजनमाहवे || 31||"

"I see no benefit in killing my own kin in battle."

Just like Arjuna, salespeople can feel this way—especially under pressure. Before a high-stakes pitch, after multiple rejections, or when self-doubt clouds the mind, their internal state collapses long before the actual challenge begins.

The Inner Storm: How the Mind Sabotages Success

In the battlefield of sales, your mind can be your best friend—or your worst enemy. One moment you're confident, and the next you're second-guessing your own voice.

Arjuna describes this precisely:

"चञ्चलं हि मनः कृष्ण प्रमाथि बलवद्दृढम् |
तस्याहं निग्रहं मन्ये वायोरिव सुदुष्करम् ||"
(Bhagavad Gita 6.34)

"The mind is restless, turbulent, powerful, and stubborn. I think it is more difficult to control than the wind."

This is the challenge every high-performing salesperson faces: the ability to maintain control of their mind in chaos. The ones who win are those who do the **inner work.**

Krishna's Response: The Art of Inner Mastery

Krishna doesn't dismiss Arjuna's fear—He acknowledges it and provides the timeless method:

"असंशयं महाबाहो मनो दुर्निग्रहं चलम् |
अभ्यासेन तु कौन्तेय वैराग्येण च गृह्यते ||"
(Bhagavad Gita 6.35)

*"O mighty-armed Arjuna, the mind is difficult to control, no doubt. But with **practice** and **detachment**, it can be conquered."*

In sales terms:

- **Practice** is the daily discipline of preparation, mindset training, goal setting, and reflection.

- **Detachment** is focusing on the process–not obsessing over the outcome.

Winners show up daily, no matter how they feel. They don't let one rejection define their identity. They master the flow of emotions and stay anchored.

Wake-Up Call: Krishna's Tough Love

When Arjuna collapses in confusion, Krishna doesn't pat his back–He challenges him:

"कुतस्त्वा कश्मलमिदं विषमे समुपस्थितम् |
अनार्यजुष्टमस्वर्ग्यमकीर्तिकरमर्जुन ||"
(Bhagavad Gita 2.2)

"Where has this weakness come from in this hour of crisis? It is unworthy of you and leads to infamy–not heaven."

"अकीर्तिं चापि भूतानि कथयिष्यन्ति तेऽव्ययाम् |
सम्भावितस्य चाकीर्तिर्मरणादतिरिच्यते ||"
(Bhagavad Gita 2.34)

"Infamy will follow you forever. For a person of honor, disgrace is worse than death."

Krishna's point is clear: Weakness comes, but we must rise above it. Leadership in sales means doing what's right, even when it's hard.

Mental Conditioning: Practical Tools to Win Within

Here's how a sales professional can train their mind:

1. **Morning Clarity Ritual** - Spend 5 minutes reviewing your goals, visualizing success, and centering your breath.
2. **Midday Reset** - After setbacks or stress, pause. Breathe. Reflect. Reframe.
3. **End-of-Day Reflection** - Write down what went well, what didn't, and what you learned. No judgment—only learning.

Add to this:

- Daily affirmations like "I am composed under pressure."
- Reading or listening to one shloka every morning.
- Short meditation before client meetings.

Chapter 19

Sales Leadership – Becoming a Rainmaker Who Inspires Others

Introduction: Leadership in Sales – From Closer to Rainmaker

A great salesperson **closes deals**–but a true rainmaker **creates an ecosystem of success**. The transition from salesperson to sales leader is not just about selling more; it's about **inspiring, coaching, and leading others to achieve greatness**.

Lord Krishna, one of the greatest leaders in history, did not fight in the Mahabharata. Instead, **he guided, inspired, and mentored warriors**, shaping the course of history. Similarly, **your role as a sales leader is not just to win but to uplift your team.**

श्रीमद्भगवद्गीता ३.२१

यद्यदाचरति श्रेष्ठस्तत्तदेवेतरो जनः |
स यत्प्रमाणं कुरुते लोकस्तदनुवर्तते ||

yad yad ācharati śhreṣhṭhas tat tad evetaro janaḥ
sa yat pramāṇaṁ kurute lokas tad anuvartate

"Whatever a great person does, others follow. The standard they set becomes the norm."

This profound wisdom reminds us that **sales leaders are role models**. Your actions, ethics, and energy **define the culture of your team**.

The Transition from Salesperson to Leader

A successful salesperson focuses on **closing deals**, but a sales leader must focus on:

✔ Inspiring their team to succeed

✔ Coaching others to improve

✔ Building a culture of excellence

✔ Leading with integrity and vision

1. Shifting from Individual Success to Team Success

Dronacharya was a master archer, but his legacy wasn't in winning battles himself–it was in **training Arjuna and other warriors**. As a sales leader, your success lies in **making others successful**.

📜 *Sales Lesson:* Stop measuring success only by **your** sales numbers. Instead, track how many people you've helped **grow and excel**.

◈ **Actionable Tip:** Start mentoring at least one junior salesperson. Guide them in overcoming objections, improving closing rates, and handling rejection.

2. The Power of Vision – Leading with Purpose

Every great leader has a **vision that inspires**. Krishna didn't just tell Arjuna to fight–he **showed him the larger purpose of dharma**.

महाभारतम् ५.१५१.२८

"नास्ति सत्यसमं तपो न सत्याद्विद्यते परम्।"

Nasti Satyasam Tapo Na Satyadwidyate Param

"There is no penance greater than truth, and nothing higher than righteousness."

📜 *Sales Lesson:* A great sales leader **doesn't just push targets**—they give their team a **purpose**. When people believe they're making a difference, they sell with conviction.

◈ **Actionable Tip:** Hold a team meeting where you define **your team's mission**. Why do you sell? What impact does your product create? Make your team believe in their **bigger purpose**.

Coaching and Mentoring Other Sales Professionals

A true rainmaker doesn't keep secrets—they share their wisdom and uplift others. Coaching is not about giving orders; it's about guiding people to unlock their potential.

1. Lord Krishna's Coaching Model: The Power of the Right Questions

Krishna didn't just **give answers** to Arjuna—he asked the right questions, leading him to **self-discovery**.

श्रीमद्भगवद्गीता २.३

क्लैब्यं मा स्म गमः पार्थ नैतत्त्वय्युपपद्यते |

klaibyaṁ mā sma gamaḥ pārtha naitat tvayyupapadyate

"Do not yield to weakness, O Partha. It does not benefit you."

Krishna's leadership wasn't about **telling** Arjuna what to do—it was about **awakening his inner warrior**.

Sales Lesson: The best sales coaches **don't just give advice—they ask powerful questions** that help salespeople find their own solutions.

◈ **Actionable Tip:** Next time a team member struggles with objections, don't just tell them what to say. Instead, ask:

✔ What do you think is stopping the client from saying yes?

✔ What has worked for you in similar situations?

✔ If you were the client, what would convince you?

This approach **empowers** your team to develop their **own critical thinking skills**.

2. Leading by Example – Walk the Talk

A leader's words mean nothing if their actions don't align. Karna was fiercely loyal to Duryodhana, not because of words, but because Duryodhana **demonstrated unwavering trust**.

Sales Lesson: If you want your team to be ethical, hardworking, and persistent, **you must embody those values yourself**.

◈ **Actionable Tip:** Make sure you:

✔ Follow up with clients **as diligently as you expect your team to**.

✔ Handle objections **without excuses**.

✔ Maintain high energy **even when sales are low**.

The Bhagavad Gita's Lessons on Transformational Leadership

The Gita is a **masterclass in leadership**. Let's extract three powerful lessons:

1. Empower Your Team, Don't Control Them

Krishna guided Arjuna but **never forced him to fight**. He gave knowledge and let Arjuna decide.

श्रीमद्भगवद्गीता १८.६३

इति ते ज्ञानमाख्यातं गुह्याद्गुह्यतरं मया |
विमृश्यैतदशेषेण यथेच्छसि तथा कुरु ||

iti te jñānam ākhyātaṁ guhyād guhyataraṁ mayā
vimṛiśhyaitad aśheṣheṇa yathechchhasi tathā kuru

"Thus, I have explained the most confidential knowledge to you. Reflect on it and act as you desire."

Sales Lesson: A great leader provides **guidance, not micromanagement**. Give your team freedom to innovate and take ownership.

◈ **Actionable Tip:** Let your team make decisions on pricing discussions, negotiation tactics, and client handling. Give them **ownership** instead of constant supervision.

2. Keep Your Team Motivated in Tough Times

Krishna **never let Arjuna give up**, even when he doubted himself.

श्रीमद्भगवद्गीता २.४७

कर्मण्येवाधिकारस्ते मा फलेषु कदाचन |

karmaṇy-evādhikāras te mā phaleṣhu kadāchana

"Your right is to perform your duty only, never to its fruits."

Sales Lesson: Teach your team to **focus on the process, not just the result**. Sales slumps happen, but persistence wins.

◈ **Actionable Tip:** When a team member is demotivated, shift their focus from missed targets to **small daily wins**—calls made, meetings set, relationships built.

3. Serve First, Lead Later

Krishna served as **Arjuna's charioteer** before leading him to victory.

Sales Lesson: A leader must be **willing to do the work first**. Be the first to make cold calls, handle tough clients, and navigate challenges.

◈ **Actionable Tip:** Spend a day doing **exactly what your sales team does**—prospecting, handling objections, following up. Let them see your **commitment**.

Actionable Steps & Assignment

☑ **Exercise 1:** Identify one salesperson in your team who is struggling. **Coach them using powerful questions** instead of direct advice.

☑ **Exercise 2:** Write down your **vision statement as a sales leader**. What culture do you want to build?

☑ **Exercise 3:** Set a personal challenge—**lead by example for one full day** by making calls, handling objections, and showing your team how it's done.

Conclusion: The Rainmaker's Legacy

A true **Rainmaker Leader** doesn't just hit targets—they **create a legacy** by inspiring others to greatness.

श्रीमद्भगवद्गीता ३.२५

सक्ता: कर्मण्यविद्वांसो यथा कुर्वन्ति भारत |
कुर्याद्विद्वांस्तथासक्तश्चिकीर्षुर्लोकसंग्रहम् ||

saktāḥ karmaṇyavidvānso yathā kurvanti bhārata
kuryād vidvāns tathāsaktaśh chikīrṣhur loka-saṅgraham

"Just as the ignorant work with attachment, so should the wise work—without attachment, for the welfare of the world."

Your leadership will be defined not by how much you sell, but by how many lives you impact.

Go forth and lead like Krishna—not just a seller, but an inspirer, a guide, and a true Rainmaker!

Chapter 20

The Ultimate Sales Playbook – Daily Habits for Continuous Growth

Introduction: Mastery is a Daily Practice

Sales isn't just about talent–it's about **discipline, consistency, and daily improvement**. The best sales performers are not those who rely on luck or natural charisma, but those who have built **strong daily habits** that keep them sharp, motivated, and at the top of their game.

Lord Krishna emphasizes the power of **continuous self-improvement** in the Bhagavad Gita:

श्रीमद्भगवद्गीता ६.१७

युक्ताहारविहारस्य युक्तचेष्टस्य कर्मसु |
युक्तस्वप्नावबोधस्य योगो भवति दुःखहा ||

yuktāhāra-vihārasya yukta-cheṣhṭasya karmasu
yukta-svapnāvabodhasya yogo bhavati duḥkha-hā

"He who is balanced in eating, sleeping, working, and recreation–such a person attains success and is free from suffering."

A great salesperson follows **structured daily rituals** that help them:

✔ Stay disciplined

✔ Maintain high energy levels

✔ Improve skills consistently

✔ Set and achieve bigger goals

Let's explore the daily habits of top sales performers, backed by ancient wisdom and modern science.

1. The Daily Rituals of Top Sales Performers

Great salespeople **don't leave success to chance**–they structure their day with intention.

1.1 The Power of a Winning Morning Routine

Ancient warriors began their day with discipline. Arjuna's guru, Dronacharya, instilled in him the habit of **early practice**, ensuring he honed his archery skills every morning.

📜 *Sales Lesson:* Your morning routine sets the tone for your entire day.

◈ Ideal Morning Habits for Sales Success:

✔ Wake up early (Brahma Muhurta - 4:00 AM to 6:00 AM is ideal for clarity and focus).

✔ Practice visualization – See yourself confidently closing deals.

✔ Read something inspiring – The Bhagavad Gita, a great sales book, or motivational content.

✔ Physical activity – Exercise boosts energy and confidence.

ऋग्वेद १०.१६८.१

"उद्बुध्यध्वं समहस्व जाग्रत प्रजायैति॥"

Udbudhyadham Samahasva Jagrat Prajaya

"Awaken, arise, and act with strength and determination."

1.2 The First Hour at Work: Preparation is Key

The **first hour at work** should not be spent on emails or distractions–it should be **dedicated to planning and preparation**.

📜 *Sales Lesson:* Winners plan their day before the day controls them.

◈ Morning Sales Ritual:

✔ Review your sales pipeline and top prospects.

✔ Set three key priorities for the day.

✔ Prepare for important meetings and calls.

✔ Listen to motivational content or sales training for 10 minutes.

This habit **keeps you ahead of the competition** and ensures you hit the ground running.

श्रीमद्भगवद्गीता २.५०

योगः कर्मसु कौशलम् ।

"Excellence in action is yoga."

Success in sales is not about **working harder**, but about **working smarter** and preparing better.

2. How to Stay Motivated and Consistent

Motivation comes and goes, but **discipline is what keeps you growing**. Even Arjuna, the greatest warrior, had moments of doubt, but Krishna **kept him focused** on his duty.

श्रीमद्भगवद्गीता ३.३०

मयि सर्वाणि कर्माणि संन्यस्याध्यात्मचेतसा |
निराशीर्निर्ममो भूत्वा युध्यस्व विगतज्वरः ||

mayi sarvāṇi karmāṇi sannyasyādhyātma-chetasā
nirāśhīr nirmamo bhūtvā yudhyasva vigata-jvaraḥ

"Surrender all your actions to me with a focused mind. Free from expectations and possessiveness, fight without anxiety."

2.1 The Science of Consistency – The 1% Rule

Sales Lesson: Getting 1% better every day leads to massive success over time.

◈ **Simple Ways to Stay Consistent:**

✓ **Set a daily learning goal** (e.g., Read one sales tip, practice a new pitch).

✓ **Make a small improvement daily** (e.g., Improve email responses, refine a script).

✓ **Track progress daily** – Small wins build confidence.

Even the Mahabharata was not won in a single battle. **It was a series of small strategic victories.**

◈ **Actionable Tip:** Keep a **Sales Journal** where you note daily learnings and improvements.

3. Tracking Progress and Setting Sales Goals

What gets **measured gets improved**. Krishna constantly reminded Arjuna of his **true purpose and larger mission**, keeping him focused.

श्रीमद्भगवद्गीता १८.१४

अधिष्ठानं तथा कर्ता करणं च पृथग्विधम् |
विविधाश्च पृथक्चेष्टा दैवं चैवात्र पञ्चमम् ||

adhiṣhṭhānaṁ tathā kartā karaṇaṁ cha pṛithag-vidham
vividhāśh cha pṛithak cheṣhṭā daivaṁ chaivātra pañchamam

"Every action consists of five factors–intention, doer, tools, execution, and divine grace."

3.1 Setting SMART Sales Goals

Sales Lesson: Clarity leads to results.

◈ **Effective Goal-Setting Framework:**

✔ **Specific** – Instead of "I want more sales," say, "I will close five deals this month."

✔ **Measurable** – Track your progress daily.

✔ **Achievable** – Set realistic but challenging targets.

✔ **Relevant** – Align goals with your long-term vision.

✔ **Time-bound** – Have deadlines to stay accountable.

महाभारतम् ५.७१.७

"संग्रामे यो विनश्यन्तं त्वरितं संधिगच्छति।
स एव प्राप्नुयात् कीर्तिं यशश्चाति विशेषतः॥"

"He who swiftly adapts in battle gains both victory and glory."

In sales, those who adapt, measure progress, and correct course always win.

◈ **Actionable Tip:** Use a **Daily Sales Tracker** to monitor leads, follow-ups, and closures.

4. The Bhagavad Gita's Wisdom on Self-Improvement

Krishna's greatest lesson was that **growth is an eternal process**–there is always a higher version of yourself to reach.

श्रीमद्भगवद्गीता ६.५

उद्धरेदात्मनात्मानं नात्मानमवसादयेत् |
आत्मैव ह्यात्मनो बन्धुरात्मैव रिपुरात्मनः ||

uddhared ātmanātmānaṁ nātmānam avasādayet
ātmaiva hyātmano bandhur ātmaiva ripur ātmanaḥ

"Elevate yourself through your own efforts. Do not degrade yourself. You are your own best friend or worst enemy."

Sales Lesson: The only competitor you need to defeat is yesterday's version of yourself.

◈ **Daily Self-Improvement Habits:**

✔ **End each day with reflection** - What went well? What can improve?

✔ **Seek feedback** - Growth comes from learning what needs fixing.

✔ **Invest in yourself** - Read, learn, and train daily.

The difference between average salespeople and top performers is the commitment to lifelong learning and improvement.

Actionable Steps & Assignments

☑ **Exercise 1:** Create a **morning routine checklist** to start your day with purpose.

☑ **Exercise 2:** Track your 1% **daily improvement** for a month. Write one thing you improved daily.

☑ **Exercise 3:** Set **SMART sales goals** for the next 30 days and monitor progress.

Conclusion: Becoming a Sales Warrior Through Daily Mastery

Success in sales is not a one-time event–it's a result of daily habits and rituals.

श्रीमद्भगवद्गीता 18.45

स्वे स्वे कर्मण्यभिरतः संसिद्धिं लभते नरः |

sve sve karmaṇy abhirataḥ sansiddhiṁ labhate naraḥ

"A person attains perfection by dedicating himself to his duty with devotion."

Sales warriors are not born; they are forged through daily discipline.

Master your habits. Master your craft. **And you will master success.**

Key Takeaways from the Book

Throughout this book, we have explored a structured yet spiritually grounded approach to mastering the art and science of sales. Here are the core principles and timeless truths that will continue to guide your path forward:

☑ **Sales is a Mindset Game:** Success in sales is 80% mindset and 20% technique. Your beliefs, self-discipline, and ability to manage rejection matter more than any script.

(**Bhagavad Gita 6.5 –**

"उद्धरेदात्मनाऽत्मानं नात्मानमवसादयेत्।" –

"One must elevate oneself through one's own mind and not degrade it.")

☑ **Purpose-Driven Goal Setting Creates Clarity:** Like Arjuna focusing only on the eye of the bird, goal clarity eliminates distractions. When your 'why' is strong, your 'how' becomes easy.

☑ **Sales Is Both an Art and a Science:** Selling is not just about intuition or charm. It's also about structure, analysis, and timing. Balance your strategy with empathy for peak performance.

✅ **Every Step of the Sales Process Matters:** From first contact to final follow-up, each stage builds the foundation of trust and value. The process, when mastered, becomes your competitive edge.

✅ **Prospecting Is Your Lifeline:** Your pipeline is your power. Regularly prospect with intention, qualify with wisdom, and follow up like a warrior on a mission.

✅ **Psychology and Storytelling Win Hearts:** Influence flows from understanding human behavior. Use stories not to sell, but to serve, guide, and inspire action.

✅ **Objection Handling Is a Growth Opportunity:** Objections are not rejections–they're signs of interest cloaked in hesitation. Handle them with empathy and presence.

✅ **Follow-Ups Create Fortune:** The fortune is in the follow-up– but only when done with persistence and patience. (Inspired by Bhagirath's relentless penance to bring the Ganga to Earth.)

✅ **Build Relationships, Not Just Revenue:** A one-time transaction is a missed opportunity. Build relationships that lead to lifetime value, referrals, and reputation.

✅ Negotiation Is About Harmony, Not Victory: True success lies in win-win outcomes. Negotiate with integrity and intention. (Mahabharata - "न चायं परजीवी स्याद्विजयी स्यात्परस्त्रिया।" - "A true victor does not thrive at the cost of another but ensures harmony in victory.")

✅ **Ethics and Dharma Are Non-Negotiable:** In a world full of shortcuts, let your values be your compass. Dharma ensures longevity, credibility, and inner peace.

✅ **Understand Customer Karma:** Not every client is meant for every product. Learn to align offerings with needs based on truth, not targets.

✅ **Money Is Energy - Respect It:** Shift from scarcity to abundance by honoring the spiritual nature of money. It flows where there's trust, value, and intention.

✅ **Tapasya Is the Secret Weapon:** Consistent action with devotion leads to greatness. Discipline is the bridge between your goals and your results.

✅ **Master the Inner Game:** Before you face the market, face yourself. Your ability to stay calm under pressure determines your real power.

✅ **Persuasion Starts with Alignment:** Influence becomes effortless when your intent is pure, your message is clear, and your energy is aligned with service.

✅ **Leaders Don't Just Perform—They Transform:** Be the Rainmaker who uplifts others. Teach, mentor, and build a legacy of empowered professionals.

✅ Habits Build Rainmakers: Daily rituals, reflection, and continuous learning forge mastery.

(Bhagavad Gita 2.50 –
"योग: कर्मसु कौशलम्" –
"Excellence in action is true yoga.")

✅ **Your Journey Is the Real Reward:** More than income or incentives, the real reward is who you become along the way—a disciplined, ethical, and deeply aware Rainmaker committed to transformation.

---

2. Applying What You've Learned in Real-World Sales

- Now that you have the knowledge, execution is key. Knowledge without action is useless, and action without strategy is ineffective. Here's how you can start applying these lessons immediately:

  📌 **Create a Personal Sales Plan:** Define your goals, daily activities, and key performance indicators (KPIs) to measure progress.

  📌 **Practice Relentlessly:** Role-play sales calls, refine your pitches, and continuously improve your approach to objections and negotiations.

  📌 **Build a Sales Journal:** Document client interactions, lessons from failures, and insights from successful deals. Learning from your experiences accelerates growth.

  📌 **Leverage Ancient Wisdom Daily:** Before key meetings or presentations, reflect on the teachings from this book—whether it's a shloka from the Bhagavad Gita or a lesson from the Ramayana—to stay grounded and focused.

  📌 **Seek Mentorship & Feedback:** Connect with experienced sales professionals, ask for feedback, and always be coachable. No matter how successful you become, there's always something new to learn.

  📌 **Stay Client-Centric:** Instead of focusing on selling, focus on solving problems for your clients. A Rainmaker is someone who genuinely cares about the success of their clients, not just their own commission.

---

3. The Lifelong Commitment to Mastery

- **Mastering sales is not a one-time achievement**—it's a lifelong pursuit. The best sales professionals are those who commit to constant learning, adaptation, and self-improvement.
- **Repetition Creates Mastery:** Keep refining your sales pitch, prospecting techniques, and negotiation skills. Never stop practicing.

(Atharva Veda –
"सत्यं वद धर्मं चर" –
"Speak the truth, walk the path of righteousness.")

- **Stay Adaptable:** Sales is always evolving. Be open to new strategies, changing consumer behaviors, and emerging technologies to stay ahead of the game.
- **Cultivate Inner Resilience:** Rejections and failures are part of the journey. Treat every NO as a lesson and every YES as a responsibility to serve your client well.

(Bhagavad Gita 18.78 –
"यत्र योगेश्वरः कृष्णो यत्र पार्थो धनुर्धरः।" –
"Where there is Krishna, the master of yoga, and Arjuna, the wielder of the bow, there lies success and victory.")

- **Teach Others & Give Back:** The final stage of mastery is sharing your knowledge. Mentor new sales professionals, write about your experiences, and contribute to the sales community. When you help others succeed, you elevate yourself.

Final Words: Become the Rainmaker You Were Meant to Be

- Sales is not just a profession—it's a way of life that demands resilience, wisdom, and continuous evolution. The true Rainmaker is one who:

✔ Leads with integrity
✔ Builds meaningful relationships
✔ Masters the art & science of selling
✔ Creates lasting impact in every deal

Now, it's time for you to go out into the world and put these lessons into action. May you sell with purpose, inspire trust, and achieve unstoppable success.

("ज्ञानं तेऽहं सविज्ञानमिदं वक्ष्याम्यशेषतः।" –
**"I shall impart to you this knowledge
with wisdom in its entirety."
- Bhagavad Gita 7.2)**

Conclusion: The Journey from Rookie to Rainmaker -

As you reach the final pages of this book, you stand at the threshold of transformation. The journey from being a rookie in sales to becoming a Rainmaker is not just about learning techniques; it's about internalizing timeless wisdom, refining your skills, and committing to continuous growth. Let's revisit the most critical takeaways that will empower you to dominate the world of sales with confidence, wisdom, and unshakable resilience.

Appendix

1. Sales Scripts and Templates

The right words at the right time can make or break a deal. Below are essential scripts and templates you can use in various sales situations. Adapt them to fit your style and industry:

1.1 Cold Calling Script

Introduction:
"Hello [Prospect's Name], this is [Your Name] from [Your Company]. I hope you're doing well. The reason for my call is that I work with professionals like you who [mention key pain points]. Many have found value in our solution, and I'd love to share how it could benefit you as well. Do you have two minutes to explore this?"

◈ *Key Tip:* Keep the opening short, engaging, and value-driven.

1.2 Follow-Up Email Template

Subject: Quick Follow-Up on Our Conversation

"Hi [Prospect's Name],

I wanted to quickly follow up on our conversation regarding [topic]. As we discussed, [reiterate a key benefit or solution].

Would love to hear your thoughts and explore the next steps. Let me know a time that works for you!

Looking forward to staying in touch.

Best,
[Your Name]"*

◈ *Key Tip*: Personalize your emails and always remind them of the value you bring.

1.3 Overcoming Objections Script

Objection: "Your product is too expensive."
Response: "I understand budget is a concern. Many of our clients felt the same way initially, but they found that our solution actually helped them [mention ROI or cost savings]. Let's explore how we can maximize the value for you."

◈ *Key Tip:* Address objections by acknowledging the concern and redirecting toward value.

More Templates:

- Closing the sale
- Asking for referrals
- Negotiation strategies

---

2. Recommended Books and Resources

To deepen your understanding of sales, psychology, and negotiation, here are some must-read books and resources:

📚 **Sales & Influence:**

- The Psychology of Selling – Brian Tracy
- SPIN Selling – Neil Rackham
- The Challenger Sale – Matthew Dixon & Brent Adamson

📚 **Negotiation & Persuasion:**

- Never Split the Difference - Chris Voss
- Influence: The Psychology of Persuasion - Robert Cialdini

📚 **Ancient Wisdom & Success:**

- *Bhagavad Gita As It Is* - A.C. Bhaktivedanta Swami Prabhupada
- *The Art of War* - Sun Tzu
- *Atomic Habits* - James Clear

📚 **Online Resources:**

- Podcasts: The Sales Evangelist, Sell or Die
- Blogs: HubSpot Sales, Sales Hacker
- YouTube Channels: Dan Lok, Grant Cardone

◈ *Key Tip:* Make reading a daily habit—even 10 pages a day can transform your sales mindset.

3. Exercises and Assignments

Mastery comes through consistent practice and application. Use these exercises to sharpen your sales skills:

3.1 Self-Reflection Exercise - The Rainmaker Mindset

- What are the three biggest sales challenges you face?
- How do you currently handle rejection? How can you improve?
- Write down your daily sales affirmations.

◈ *Key Tip:* Mindset shapes results—train yourself to think like a Rainmaker.

3.2 Prospecting Challenge

- Make a list of 20 high-quality prospects you haven't contacted yet.
- Craft a personalized outreach strategy (call, email, LinkedIn message).
- Track responses and refine your approach.

◈ *Key Tip:* The more you prospect, the better your pipeline.

3.3 Objection Handling Roleplay

- Pair up with a colleague or practice in front of a mirror.
- List the top 5 objections you face.
- Respond to each as if you were in a real sales conversation.

◈ *Key Tip:* Rehearse until your responses become second nature.

3.4 30-Day Rainmaker Challenge

Week 1: Mastering Prospecting – Connect with 10 new potential clients.
Week 2: Storytelling & Pitching – Refine your sales presentation.
Week 3: Objection Handling – Face objections head-on with confidence.
Week 4: Closing & Referrals – Ask for business and referrals assertively.

◈ *Key Tip:* Track progress daily—small improvements lead to massive results.

Final Words from the Appendix

This section is meant to be your sales toolkit—whenever you face a challenge, come back to these scripts, books, and exercises. The real secret to success is consistent action, self-improvement, and lifelong learning.

◈ *Key Takeaway:* A true Rainmaker is not someone who simply closes deals but someone who inspires trust, builds relationships, and creates long-term success.

Your Next Step:
Go out and apply these lessons immediately. Sales success is not about what you know, but what you implement. Now, take action and become the Rainmaker you were meant to be!

www.ingramcontent.com/pod-product-compliance
Lightning Source LLC
LaVergne TN
LVHW041945070526
838199LV00051BA/2908
9789370183827